MW01538516

GOD'S PRESENCE

AN EYEWITNESS ACCOUNT

TONY A TRAN

Revision number 1, April 2024

ISBN: 979-8-9892777-0-4 (eBook - Kindle)

ISBN: 979-8-9892777-1-1 (Hardcover)

ISBN: 979-8-9892777-2-8 (Paperback)

Library of Congress Control Number: 2023918879

God's Presence

DEDICATION

To God the Father, to God the Son, and to God the Holy Spirit

CONTENTS

Preface

Just a few months ago, my life was seemingly finally going down a secure path. After more than a decade of ups and downs, I worked in a stable professional job for three years.

Although the job was very taxing, along with the associated risk of physical harm, I was able to make good money and survive the bad economy. I was looking to accumulate enough money to possibly buy a nice house, start a family, or be successful in some side business ventures.

But truly, who controls our lives? Did we decide when we were going to come into this world or which family we wanted to be born into? Did we decide that we would get whatever we wanted in life? Or what would be true?

I am now unemployed. I am writing this to you because of what happened to me. Something unexpected, even by a stretch of my imagination, had happened. **I had met the living God in person, and various miracles occurred**.

It is a long story, and you may wonder whether it is real or even possible. I lay down in this book my life story leading to the appointment with God. I recall as accurately as possible the relevant events for you to examine. It is up to you to use the information in this book for your benefit.

For me, God revealed Himself to me, so I became His witness. It was clear from our encounter that whether I live or die at any moment is squarely in God's hand. I am His slave, and my job is to testify to the truth.

Acknowledgments

I am grateful to my parents for raising me to adulthood and providing some early information in this book that I did not know or forgot about. I am grateful to my father, who has always supported and invested in my endeavors. I am grateful to my paternal grandmother, who has always cared for and prayed for me whenever possible.

I am grateful to all my family members, friends, teachers, colleagues, and various people who have impacted and shaped the experiences that I had throughout my life journey. In addition, I am thankful to the communities of believers in Buffalo, New York, and in the Twin Cities, Minnesota, through which I have experienced grace, love, and mercy from God.

Early Childhood

Born Into This World

I have been wondering about this mysterious experience to this day. Do you remember when your consciousness began? Was it when you were three months old, or the day you were born? I did not know about the world and the life that we all are living right now. All I knew was darkness and nothingness.

Also, this darkness and nothingness had no end; it had been going on forever. I remember thinking to myself (yes, I knew what I was thinking), where is this darkness and nothingness going? What will happen next? If that 'next' will ever come? After so long, I eventually gave up hope for a change, but then I saw the light in the darkness. Then, the light shed away all of the darkness, and I was born into this world.

I remember there were lights, sounds, and creatures surrounding me. The creatures looked at me cheerfully with a pleasing countenance. They said something to me that I did not understand. As it turned out, they were my family members during my childhood, and they spoke in Vietnamese, which I only learned to understand later.

According to my family, I was named Trần Anh Tuấn, and I was born on November 25, 1980, the lunar year of the Metal Monkey, in Hanoi city, the capital of the Socialist Republic of Vietnam.

Family and Life

My mother, father, grandmother, and aunt lived in a roughly 20-square-meter room allocated by the government within a large villa at 5 Phan Boi Chau Street, downtown Hanoi. The room was too small for a family, so a crawling loft was made within the room as an additional sleeping space.

There were separate places for bathing and toileting shared with many other families living within the villa. People used metal buckets and masonry tanks to store water from one main water line along the entranceway. Water was boiled in a kettle and then stored in thermoses for hot water needs. My family and everyone else lived a poor and simple life. We had boiled rice, boiled water spinach, and fish sauce for regular meals. Sometimes, we had pork and other things, but they were very limited in quantity. We were living under a socialist economy in which the government allotted each family the required necessities of life. People worked six days a week and only had an off on Sundays.

I was taught that my family had no religion, but like other families, we had the tradition of 'ancestor worship.' Quality fruits and food were placed on an altar table with burning *nag champa* on certain occasions. Then my grandmother would pray, and we would wait until all the *nag champa* burned off before we could eat the food and the fruits.

The government advocated that each family should only have 1 to 2 children due to the concern regarding excessive population growth, and I was the only child of my parents.

An average family had one bicycle and had to wait a long time to receive a spare tire or a bar of soap. We had electricity for light bulbs, but the electricity went out very often. A kerosene stove was used for cooking, and a kerosene lamp was used for light when electricity was lost in the evenings.

My father's name was Trần Văn Thanh, and he was born in Thanh Hoa province in 1953. He worked as a lecturer at the Hanoi University of Mining and Geology. My mother's name was Hà Thị Oanh, and she was born in Bac Giang province in 1955. She worked as a journalist at Ha Noi Moi Newspaper. My father and mother met during their college years studying abroad in Romania and married in Hanoi in 1979.

My paternal grandfather's name was Trần Văn Đối, and he was born in Vinh Phuc province in 1925. He died as an Army company commander of the Vietnamese military in a battle at Non Nuoc Mountain, Ninh Binh province in 1953, just before my father's birth during the First Indochina War.

Officially, my paternal grandmother's name was Nguyễn Thị Minh Hải; she was born in Bac Ninh province in 1928 and worked as a pharmaceutical staff at Viet Duc Hospital. However, I was told by family members that she was born a few years earlier with a different name at birth and never married. My aunt was her younger daughter from another father who was a military officer during the Vietnam War.

Vivid Memories

I lived happily because family members were close to me all the time. The neighboring families were next door, and there were children of various ages whom I played with. My father made my wooden toys, and my grandmother always fed me the best available food.

My memories of my father include events like when he was sleeping in bed on his stomach after drinking alcohol with friends. He started feeling hot and pulled down his pants, exposing his buttocks. I saw that and pulled his pants back up. My father pulled it down again; then, I pulled it back up again. I was about two years old and did this without prior knowledge or understanding.

I also have shared certain experiences with my grandmother that are etched vividly in my mind. Once, I saw some household items vibrating strangely and asked my grandmother what was happening. She told me that it was an earthquake. Vietnam is a country not known to have an earthquake, and that has been the only one I have experienced myself to this day.

I do not recall being taken care of well by my mother. Even she admitted once she splashed a bucket of cold water on me because I had pooped myself as a baby, and then I became very sick because of the cold water. My grandmother also told me that once, I wanted the grapefruit that my mother was eating, but she did not give it to me, so my grandmother bought it for me instead. I remember being left alone on the street during nursery school a couple of times because my mother forgot to pick me up after the school had closed.

As strange as it sounds, I was not an innocent toddler at nursery school either. In our school, during nap time, boys and girls were left sleeping next to each other, wearing pants with holes for peeing. I would use my hand to play with the genitals of the girl sleeping next to me. At the time, I wasn't aware that it was wrong. I was curious and seeking pleasure.

A few times, my mother brought me to visit her original family in Long Tri village within the Yen Dung district of Bac Giang province, about 65 kilometers from Hanoi city, where people mostly had been living and had self-sufficient lives.

Each family had buffalos and farmland to grow and harvest rice crops, a large garden with a fish pond, various fruit trees, chicken flocks, and other domesticated animals and livestock.

Water was obtained from a deep well for daily use. There was no electricity, a metal wood-burning grate was used for cooking, and a kerosene lamp was used for light in the evenings.

Many large bamboo bushes, along with mud and bricks, were utilized as building materials. This was how roughly 90 percent of the Vietnamese population lived. My mother is the oldest child of my maternal grandparents. Along with her, there are four sisters and one brother.

Vestiges of War

The Vietnamese people during this time loved and worshiped the late Uncle Ho, whose official name was Ho Chi Minh. He was regarded as the founding father of the country and the people. Under Uncle Ho's leadership, the northern Vietnamese people emerged victorious from the First Indochina War against France and victorious again from the Vietnam War against the United States.

My family brought me to visit Uncle Ho's Mausoleum a few times, where people had to wait in a very long line to see his preserved body in a glass case. Vietnamese people and my family believed in Marxist-Leninist ideology indoctrinated by the Communist Party of Vietnam, the country's only political party.

Many Vietnamese people died, and many homes and infrastructures in Hanoi city were destroyed due to the Vietnam War. There was a family in Kham Thien Street where everyone died without leaving a trace from a B-52 bombing on December 26, 1972.

Agent Orange, an herbicide and defoliant chemical, was sprayed by the U.S. military over the vast agricultural lands of Vietnam. It caused forest defoliation, sharply reduced animal species, and caused severe congenital disabilities in the children born to the people exposed to it. It was fortunate that none of my immediate family members died during the Vietnam War.

Nevertheless, the sentiment of the people and my family was that the United States was an enemy and an evil empire, and they disregarded innocent lives because of their political purposes.

New Home and Life

In 1985, my father went to Moscow, the Soviet Union, for his graduate study. My mother and I moved to Ngoc Ha village and lived in a newly built house that belonged to my uncle, my mother's only brother.

The house was now number 78, niche 63, lane 173, Hoang Hoa Tham Street, Hanoi city. It was one of the neighborhood's few brick homes with a flat concrete top. The house consisted of living space, sleeping space, a crawling loft, an attached kitchen, and an attached toilet and bathroom, totaling roughly 60 square meters.

The house had a large water tank to accumulate water for daily usage and a stairway to the flat rooftop used for hanging and drying clothes. We also had electricity and a small black and white television (TV). It was a lot more comfortable space-wise compared to where I previously lived.

However, the neighbors were strangers, few in number, and enclosed within fences made of hibiscus bushes. My uncle was out of the house all the time, so I rarely saw him, and my mother was also at work until the evenings, so I was home alone most of the time.

One late evening, I woke up from sleep and noticed my mother was not with me. I found her lying on the floor with a strange man. I did not understand what was happening and was not happy even though my mother explained this stranger was her friend. My mother also told me that I was born out of her armpit. I did not know why she told me so, but I believed her.

Around this time, the government started adopting Saturdays as a day off, along with Sundays. I was brought to visit my paternal grandmother regularly and to Viet Xo Friendship Labor Cultural Palace in downtown Hanoi, where I learned pencil sketching and Karate for one summer.

I also started to know other kids my age living in Ngoc Ha village and assimilated to walking on dirt roads and playing in flower fields. Various natural drainage trenches were flowing across the town and a main water line area from which clean water was carried via large buckets and shoulder poles into an individual home's water tank.

I recall that not many of my neighbors and kids were friendly, but I found two good boys whose homes were next to each other and not far away from where I lived. Trung, who was one year younger than me, and Hải, who was my age with the same name as my paternal grandmother. Hải's parents also got to know and became friends with my mother.

Since I had to be enrolled in elementary school, my mother taught me to read Vietnamese and do basic arithmetic a little earlier to prepare me for elementary school. I was a good student and a quick learner, so I learned to read and do basic arithmetic relatively easily.

School Days

School and Learning

I started attending the Ba Dinh School on Hoang Hoa Tham Street in 1986. It was one of the Elementary and Middle schools closest to where I lived. I remember my mother brought me to meet the principal, who had a wooden arm covered in his shirt sleeve. I embarrassed my mother because I kept asking, "*Where is the amputee teacher?*" because a neighbor kid had told me the principal was an amputee, and I did not recognize him.

I was accepted to class 1A, and after being brought to and picked up from school for a while, my mother let me walk to school and back home on my own.

The school had a large five-story brick building for classrooms and teacher's offices. A classroom had an array of long wooden desks, each consisting of five drawers and a wooden bench for five pupils. The floor of the front area of the class was elevated and had a brick table with a stone top and a chair for the teacher. The blackboard was green and embossed into the front wall of the class. Above the blackboard was a portrait photo of the late Uncle Ho with white hair, mustache, and beard, and a sign written with his five teachings, "*Love the homeland; love the homeland people; study well; work well; humble, honest, courageous.*"

I did very well in school and always got a mark of 10, the highest grade in the schooling system, for my reading, writing, spelling, and arithmetic skills because my mother had already taught me in advance. Every pupil carried on hand an ink pen put inside an inkpot with a handle, and on the back a briefcase with notebooks and books. The favorite book I brought to class for oral examination of reading skills was '*The Ant and the Pigeon*' by Leo Tolstoy, which was bound in beautiful glossy papers and filled with color images. This book was one of the few Russian books translated into Vietnamese and printed in the Soviet Union that I got from my mother.

My father also sent me beautiful and amazing toys from the Soviet Union. I was very impressed with everything made in that foreign country; they were clearly of a different world with advanced technology and knowledge.

However, the people living in the village were generally not educated or civilized; brawling, swearing, bullying, and theft often occurred in the village, which sometimes happened to my family. My mother also taught me how to help with cooking and washing the dishes; however, she still treated me badly once in a while by knocking on my head with her knuckles if I made a mistake or woke her up from her nap during noon time.

As a child, I was told folklore about unfortunate children or mistreated people who cried out during periods of desperation in their lives. Then, a deity appeared to comfort them. Another thing I kept noticing, at the start of Phan Boi Chau Street across the road, there was a large pharmaceutical store with a snake scepter emblem. It felt mysterious and strange to me how that symbolizes healing pills.

Economic Changes

In 1986, The Communist Party of Vietnam initiated economic reforms called Renovation that sought to transition Vietnam from a command economy to a socialist-oriented market economy.

I was still brought to visit my paternal grandmother during the weekends. She had retired and raised pigs at a corner of the villa and brewed alcohol secretly at home to earn money. My father also sent merchandise from the Soviet Union, and most of them were sold for profit. Because of these, my family's living conditions improved; we had electrical stoves, old fridges, and other household items imported from the Soviet Union.

Since my family's living conditions had improved, my parents could arrange music lessons for me. I was taught how to play the Mandolin along with some other kids by a musician who was a next-door neighbor at 5 Phan Boi Chau Street. I performed very well and better than the other kids, and that made me excessively proud.

I was often home by myself; luckily, my mother brought home books regularly, and I read them in my free time. In contrast to the few imported Russian books, these were Chinese novels translated into Vietnamese and printed locally. The papers were thin, brown, and of low quality and defects. However, the stories were very captivating to my curiosity and imagination.

Spiritual Novel

'*Journey to the West*' was one of the prominent novels that span multiple volumes. In its story, this monkey king was born of stone and learned magical abilities from a mysterious deity. He was so powerful, wielding a rod of iron, and rebelled against the empire and emperor of heaven. However, he was defeated and locked up under a mountain by

Buddha. He was later freed to escort a Buddhist monk on a trip to the West to obtain Buddhist sacred texts. On the journey, he defeated and recruited two other fallen officers of heaven who incarnated in the form of a pig-man and Satan. The pig-man's bad characters and fleshly temptations brought them many troubles with different magical monsters or evil magicians. The monkey king had to fight hard to overcome every time, and often with help from other bodhisattvas or Taoist sages and deities. When they got to the final destination, they were given empty texts and had to bribe the gatekeepers to obtain genuine sacred texts. After 17 years, the group finally completed the journey and came back. The monkey king was granted Buddhahood and titled Fight and Defeat the Buddha.

Visiting the Soviet Union

In the summer of 1987, my father arranged a trip for my paternal grandmother and me to visit him in Moscow, where he was doing his graduate study. It was the first time I rode in a car, a Lada made in the Soviet Union, on the way to the airport. It was also the first time I flew on an airplane; it was so big and intimidating. The flight was more than a day long, with several stops and delays, and I had motion sickness the whole time.

My father lived in an apartment with his roommate in a high-rise building, and there was a spare bed for my grandmother and me. The building also had a garden with apples and wild cats and a soccer field. Life here was so different, and I felt like I was living in a heavenly world. It was the first time I saw and operated an elevator, the first time I saw the common kitchen room and many gas stoves for the whole building floor. The first time I saw and mistakenly sat backward on the modern toilet. Everything was bigger in size, different in color or taste, or how it worked in an amazing way: the people, animals, trees, fruits, foods, and buildings.

My father brought my grandmother and me on buses to visit different places in Moscow, including amusement parks, museums, Red Square, and the underground metro system. The metro was large and beautiful. There were three levels. It was built like an underground city with a dome ceiling that goes anywhere in the Moscow metropolitan area and even travels through the Volga River. We also traveled on a train to Leningrad, which was originally and presently Saint Petersburg, and visited the Hermitage Museum and Palaces of the historical Russian Emperors. There were breathtaking paintings, sculptures, wildlife, and scenery everywhere I went.

One night, my father and I visited one of my father's female friends, and we stayed at her place overnight. I woke up during the night because I heard her say, "*Hurting my neck...*" and I saw two people moving together, fully covered with a blanket in her bed. I knew they were doing something not right, but she treated me well, and I was happy with everything, so I ignored it and kept sleeping.

At that time, everything in the Soviet Union had a fixed price, and the price was even embossed on the items wherever possible. I was fascinated and loved the various electric, mechanical, and even programmable toys my father bought me. It was also the first time I saw a home video game system, the Nintendo Entertainment System, and played Super Mario Bros and Duck Hunt.

Our Own House

In 1989, my father returned to Vietnam for a short time to oversee the construction of our new house just across a flower field from my uncle's house. My uncle also got married during this time, and there was not enough living space for my parents and me, so we moved to live temporarily in a small apartment in Nghia Do, a district of Hanoi. After our new house was constructed, my mother and I moved to live there in 1990.

The house is now located at number 221, lane 158, Ngoc Ha Street, Hanoi City, where my mother still lives until now. The house was a two-story brick building of around 140 square meters. It had a porch, living room, bathroom, kitchen, and dining room on the first floor. Two bedrooms, a reading room, and a balcony were located on the second floor of the house. The windows and other woodwork were done by my friend Hải's father, a skilled carpenter. There was a small garden and walkway around the house. We also got a waterline, an electrical pump to accumulate water into water tanks, and other household items and appliances imported from the Soviet Union.

Early Middle School

I graduated Elementary school from class 1A to 5A with the highest honors. I was admitted to the Ho Chi Minh Communist Pre-Youth Union, where I needed to wear a specifically designed red scarf when going to school.

One day, out of curiosity of my growing mind, I asked my mother where human beings were from. My mother answered that according to the religion of Christianity, the original human ancestors were Adam and Eve, whom God created. I was a little surprised at her answer since my family does not follow any religion, and it was understood that religions are not truths but ancient, superstitious beliefs.

I was accepted to class 6B at the start of Middle school. Later, I realized that class 6A was a selected class for better teaching and curriculum. To be admitted to A class, I needed to take a competitive exam that I did not know about. I also discovered that typically, a pupil must do additional math and literature classes in the evening to do well in class, and the parents pay for these.

One of my additional classes' locations was at a small school looking to the B-52 Lake near my house, where a main portion of the shot-down B-52 bombing aircraft was still stationed. In the Hanoi Botanical Garden adjacent to Ngoc Ha village, there were other portions of the shot-down B-52 aircraft, where my friends and I usually played soccer using a plastic ball on the asphalt roads.

I remember Trung, I, and another neighbor friend went to a big lake of the Botanical Garden one day during the summer, and we caught a lot of water snails to bring to my new house and boiled them for a great, delicious meal. My mother's youngest sister came to live with us in our new house to study for her university entrance exams. She and I were paid by my mother to take Karate classes on a tennis court of a sports club, where I earned my Green belt after a year and a half.

The pupils at Middle School had to line up according to their classes in the schoolyard and sing the national anthem before being allowed to enter classrooms. There was a break at half-time, and the pupils had to perform a routine physical exercise in the schoolyard following school drum signals. Somehow, I was chosen to be trained and to perform school drum signals during the break.

I was one of the top two pupils in mathematics in my class at the end of the year, and the lead teacher, a literature teacher, asked us to help her calculate the grade point averages. After we calculated the averages, the other pupil decided to mark our grades even higher than they were; I knew this was wrong but agreed with him out of the temptation for recognition.

Many Nintendo Entertainment Systems were imported into Vietnam during this time. Various families bought these systems and rented them out inside their houses to the neighboring kids for about 800 Vietnamese Dong per hour. I got a mini bicycle from my mother and learned how to ride it. I used the bicycle to travel around and visit my paternal grandmother on weekends. And whenever I visited my paternal grandmother, I immediately asked her for some money to play video games at these rental places. It became my habit and addiction, and I started to steal money from my grandmother's purse to buy more playtime.

Selective Class

Being aware of the competitiveness of the schooling system and how it affects the future, our parents paid for Hải and me to attend additional mathematics classes at Hanoi-Amsterdam High School for the Gifted for a short time. After finishing class 7B, one of my classmates and I requested to take the competitive exams for class A entrance. I was the one who performed well enough to be admitted to class 8A, replacing one previous female pupil who heart-wrenchingly cried when this happened to her.

Being two years behind in the selected teaching and curriculum, I struggled in my class and performed near the bottom at the beginning. However, I made friends and learned from other pupils in the class and got better. My school also received the bad news that my previous class 6B and 7B math teacher died from being electrocuted while he was trying some repairs. The electrical voltage in Vietnamese households was 220.

During this time, my aunt, who lived with my paternal grandmother at 5 Phan Boi Chau Street, got married. My uncle-in-law was an officer at the Ministry of Foreign Affairs. He bought two additional rooms from neighbors within the villa, one as an extension to the original room and the other a few steps away. Trung, I, and other local kids started playing video games regularly at a popular place in Ngoc Ha village. And I used the money for meals and additional classes to pay for the video game play time.

Diplomatic Normalization

In 1994, my father returned to Vietnam permanently when I was a pupil in class 9A, the last year of Middle School. One day my father asked me to show him my penis and its condition to see if I needed to be circumcised, but it was fine and I have never been circumcised to this day. I remember my father brought me twice to a nationally respected retired math teacher and asked him to train me, but he refused both times.

That same year, The United States lifted its 30-year trade embargo on Vietnam. And in 1995, after a 20-year hiatus of severed ties, President Bill Clinton announced the formal normalization of diplomatic relations between the United States of America and the Socialist Republic of Vietnam. Due to the rise of the U.S.'s economic, political and military power, and the improvement in Vietnamese people's living standards since economic reforms in 1986, more and more Vietnamese people started to have favorable views of the U.S.

I performed well in school and made good friends with Sơn, one of the best pupils in my class within my small group. Then I graduated from Middle School with honors and high enough graduation exam points to be admitted directly to a High School according to my parents' residence registration without taking the entrance exams.

High School Days

Selective Examinations

According to my mother's residence registration, made when we lived in Nghia Do, I was admitted directly to branch A of Yen Hoa High School on Nguyen Khang Street, Cau Giay District. It was known as a good school within its district but somewhat far away from my house compared to Chu Van An High School, one of the three national high schools for the gifted in Vietnam. I wanted to go to Chu Van An, but the school did not accept direct admission and required competitive examinations.

During this time, high school classes in Vietnam were experimentally divided into branches; Branch A emphasized natural science, Branch B emphasized technical skills, and Branch C emphasized social science. I registered for the competitive examinations of branch A of Chu Van An and took additional mathematics classes at the school during the summer of 1995 to prepare for its entrance examination.

It was during these additional mathematics classes that I met my first and serious crush. Her name was Thư. She graduated from a different middle school and was also admitted directly to her local high school. Out of inexperience and natural attraction to her, I initiated contact confidently via paper messages, to which she responded positively. Thư was the smartest and most attractive girl I had known then, and I fell for her quickly. However, she did not fall for me as she had some previous romantic experiences.

My crush on Thư and the start of my puberty seemed to coincide. She fully captured my thoughts and imagination. I idealized having a successful romance and serious relationship with her. However, the reality was the opposite of what I expected.

I underperformed in the mathematics exam and performed poorly in the literature exam. As a result, I was not admitted to Chu Van An High School. On the other hand, Thư did better than me and was admitted and then enrolled in Chu Van An. I was devastated because I lost the chance to see and be around my crush at school.

Soon after, I also underperformed in the required mathematics exam for admission to the selected 10A1 class of Yen Hoa High School. And therefore, I was assigned to the 10A2 class. Knowing that my true abilities were at the level of the selected 10A1 class, I talked about it with my mother. To my surprise, my mother knew someone at the school, and by the beginning of the school year, I was reassigned to the 10A1 class. I was also given a new full-size bicycle to travel to school and back.

External Influences

To my surprise, Thư and her family subsequently moved to a house in Ngoc Ha village, just a short walk from my house, and I saw her in the prime of her beauty from time to time. My infatuation with her intensified, and I tried foolishly to contact her via letters and sometimes went to her house, but she avoided me. Somehow, I still kept very strong belief that eventually I would win her over, and my idealization of having a lifetime relationship with her would happen.

My mother would still bring new books home and put them in the reading room. I read most of the books available out of curiosity and because there were no other choices for me. There were scientific books written for lay people from the Soviet Union and translated into Vietnamese. Those books captured and fascinated my intellectual mind.

One of my favorites from those books was '*Astronomy for Entertainment.*' It described in detail the Big Bang theory, how the universe came into existence, the size and behavior of stars, galaxies, black holes, and other phenomena working in the universe. On the other hand, there were also translated novels, magazines, and non-fiction written by American authors.

I remember a very thick Almanac called '*The Mother and The Beauty Faction.*' It had many glossy color photos of Western and American women exposing their bodies, including nude pictures. American novels also always included explicit details of the sexual relationships of characters who were not married. These sexual relationships were not depicted as morally wrong but as something natural and passionate living.

I also first obtained from an acquaintance a Video Home System tape cassette recording of pornography originating from the United States and watched it secretly at home. It was during this time that I started to masturbate, and it became a way that I used to release sexual simulation or tension.

After school and meals, I almost always rode my bicycle to the popular place for playing video games in the village. I played with Trung and a few other regulars. We had good times and fellowship, which I severely lacked at home. The video game system rented out at this place had progressed from the Nintendo Entertainment System to the Sega Genesis to the Super Nintendo Entertainment System. So, the playing fee increased to 1200 Vietnamese Dong per hour. The games became more complicated, intellectually challenging, and took longer to finish, especially the Japanese games I was attracted to. The players had to save their game progress on a floppy disk, and it would take weeks or even months to finish a game.

I spent more time playing video games and for a longer duration than before, and to have the money, I started stealing money that my parents kept in their bedroom's wardrobe. My parents did not like my gaming obsession; however, they were not home most of the time, so I continued gaming and neglected to study.

Once in a while, my father would bring me to visit his female friend, whom I mentioned during my Moscow visit in the past. Her husband had died, and she had returned to Vietnam and lived in Hanoi with her only daughter. It was also strange to me that a few times, my mother talked about how my family's house and property would be divided should my parents get divorced.

Spiritual Video Game

There was this masterpiece turn-based role-playing game freshly came out of Japan called '*Fire Emblem: Genealogy of the Holy War*' with majestic music, mesmerizing characters, and a complex storyline of medieval battles, romance, chivalry, magic, and evil. The player controlled a party of characters to travel, fight enemies, and conquer fortresses over vast terrains.

The game got exceedingly harder as one proceeded, but I played it patiently and as perfectly as possible using many game resets and different trials and errors. I left no team members dead and leveled all of them up powerfully. Like a game of my soul, I instinctively knew secret places for holy weapons and recruited all recruitable characters. At the end of the 5th chapter of the game, I was devastated that after winning all the hard-fought battles over the continent, my team returned home in celebration just to be deceived into a dead end surrounded by betrayed allies and was ruthlessly slaughtered. Even worse, my main character was executed by the holy fire after being shown that his wife's memory was forcefully erased, and she had become the wife of the holy fire wielder.

The game seemed to end after that, showing the storyline in texts and memoirs of passed-away characters. Still, then, a new chapter began with new territories and new characters. Most of them were the children of the previous generation.

I continued to play diligently and got to the final chapter, where the daughter of the holy fire wielder and the original wife of my first-generation main character came to attack my team non-stop. Her face was sad, and her eyes were red. Sensing something unusual, I commanded my team not to fight back or to hurt her and then killed a magician of darkness at the far corner of the continent. After the magician of darkness was killed, her eyes were no longer red, and I let my main character talk to her and successfully recruited her to my team. Then I let her come to the conquered fortress of the magician of darkness. There, she found the tome of Holy Light, the only weapon to defeat the Dark God, who was a dragon and the game's final boss.

At the time, other good players were also playing the game ahead of me. However, their team suffered casualties, and they did not recruit all possible characters or missed out on holy weapons. One player came to the final stage way ahead of me. He did not let the girl with red eyes live, and none of his characters could deal damage to the Dark God, so he also gave up.

I was the first to find the Holy Light, defeat the Dark God and finish the game. For this reason, the owner of the video game rental place awarded me nine free playing hours. It was unexpected and unprecedented among the circle of players there.

Unusual Connections

During this period, there was rising corruption in the Vietnamese government systems, organizations, and institutions. Bribery was commonly accepted as a means of doing business and seeking advancement. It was understood that there were power struggles and infightings among factions of the Communist Party. There were members of the Communist Party of Vietnam who were caught and convicted of serious criminal charges. I remember a head of the Vietnamese special operation against drug dealing was convicted of dealing a mass amount of illegal drugs himself and was sentenced to death.

During my school break times, somehow, I got into conversations with a student of the same year but from a different class. His name was Thủy, and we had a connection like that of soulmates. It was strange that even though we were not in the same class and rarely met, I maintained my friendship with Thủy better than any student in my class.

Relative to my A1 classmates, I performed reasonably well in mathematics and physics but poorly in chemistry and literature since I had no interest in these subjects. I spent most of my free time playing video games at the same popular place in Ngoc Ha village and was considered aloof in personality by some of my classmates. Nevertheless, I was a decent student overall and was admitted to the Ho Chi Minh Communist Youth Union, just like most high school students in Vietnam.

During previous years, my mother learned another foreign language: French. And for a year, from 1995 to 1996, she went to live in Paris, France, as part of her professional study in journalism under a scholarship she had won with Thomson Reuter. She made good friends with the landlord's family, where she stayed. In 1998, the landlord's family in Paris came to Hanoi and visited my family. We had a good time together, and the landlord lady first called and gave me the name *Tony*.

Preparation for University Entrance Exams

There was extremely high pressure on high school students and their parents to prepare early for university entrance exams. Admittance to a respected university was considered necessary for anyone wishing for a bright future. The universities in Vietnam were primarily concentrated in the two largest cities, Hanoi, the Capitol, and Ho Chi Minh City, in the southern part of Vietnam.

Each university specialized in only one broad field of discipline and administered its own entrance exams for admissions. To increase the likelihood of scoring better in the university entrance exams, the students needed additional training classes all year round and as early as possible. Special training classes were concentrated in the cities, tailored to styles and contents that closely resemble the entrance exams of a specific university. Families from provinces far away had to send their sons and daughters to live in rental places or with relatives, just like my mother's youngest sister did in the past, to attend these special training classes.

I was not that interested in these because something seemed wrong to me. Why were there undue troubles and unhealthy pressures on the students? Why did families spend all their money on training classes for their children just because of a few exams that will be forgotten immediately after?

However, there was the expectation of an educated family and myself that I would go to university. My father hired different tutors to help me study physics, chemistry, and mathematics. Most of them were current students in university who specialized in each discipline. Sometimes, my father also brought me to a special training class organized by his university's faculty members.

My father's investment in my training did help me to improve my performance in school, especially in physics, as the subject genuinely interested me because it was related to real-life phenomena. I was selected to the physics team of my school the last two years to attend a competition exam for students in Hanoi city, but that was it. I had no interest in chemistry, did not really study it, and performed poorly in the subject. I was somewhat interested in mathematics, but it seemed the subject was all about knowing the right tricks, methods, and transformations.

In biology class, it was taught that humans originated from the ape and that all living things were formed through a gradual process of evolution over millions of years. It sounded weird to me that humans came from the ape, a current living animal seen in the zoo. However, I accepted it as the only truth that had an explanation of human origin, and because everyone believed in it and told me so.

Selection of University Major

I asked my father for advice regarding which university to apply to. Initially, he suggested the University of Finance and Accountancy. Later, he recommended a career in civil engineering, or in geology and mining, the discipline he was a faculty member of.

A student was allowed to register for three universities. So, I selected the Civil Engineering major at the National University of Civil Engineering and at Hanoi Architectural University, and the Petroleum major at Hanoi University of Mining and Geology which was very popular and competitive with the prospect of a high-earning career.

In the summer of 1998, I completed the high school graduation exams and graduated with minimal honors. In contrast to Middle School, what mattered to high school students were not graduation grades and points but their performance on the university entrance exams of their choice. During that time, I still kept spending minimal time studying and a lot of time playing video games, as they were my true interest.

Without much practice in exam-taking skills, I underperformed in the university entrance exams relative to my abilities. Fortunately, my good performance in physics earned me enough points to be accepted to the Civil Engineering department of the Hanoi Architectural University. My performance was also far from enough to be admitted to the Petroleum Department of Hanoi University of Mining and Geology. To my surprise, my father suggested he could get me accepted into the Land Surveying department instead. It was clear that personal connections with the universities could influence the admission process.

My good friend, Hải, had been training in pencil sketching and had selected Architecture as his university major. He had applied to the National University of Civil Engineering and Hanoi Architectural University. Unfortunately, he did not perform well enough to be accepted to either university. So, he continued his study and training to take the entrance exams again the following year.

University Days

Class Structure

In August 1998, I started attending Hanoi Architectural University as a Civil Engineering student of class 98X5. The university was located in the Ha Dong district of Hanoi, somewhat far away from my house, so my father bought me a new gas motorcycle for transportation. A motorcycle was an extremely popular means of transportation for people and was also considered a symbol of looks, wealth, and style for young people.

My university class was different because only a few students were from Hanoi, and a big chunk of students hailed from other provinces within northern Vietnam. Those students had to rent a living place surrounding the university or live at a nearby relative's house. Several students were accepted to the class after their second or third attempts on the university entrance exams and were older than others. Also, there were only two female students in the class as the whole university had a very low percentage of them.

The political system in Vietnam had two parallel leadership roles: the government officials and the Communist Party officials. The latter was the de facto governing power, and all government officials were members of and assigned by the Party. This parallel was implemented in almost all organizations and institutions and also applied to university students. Each university class had one monitor and two vice-monitors as the governing branch, one secretary and two committee members or vice-secretaries as the political branch. In the first year, the university selected the leaders of a class according to unknown criteria. Therefore, I became a member of my class Communist Youth Union Committee.

Video Game Hobby

In those days, there was an increase in imported personal computers (PC) and computer components from overseas. And my father bought me my first PC ever. I was fascinated with computer technology and reconnected with Sơn, the brilliant friend in my small group since Middle School. Sơn went to the Information Technology class of Hanoi-Amsterdam High School for the Gifted. He won a national competition prize and was admitted directly to the Information Technology Department of the Hanoi University of Science and Technology. With Sơn's help and pointers, I learned to type with ten fingers and managed and maintained my PC very well. Sơn and I also participated in a Taekwondo practice club for a few months. There, I recalled my previous Karate skills and assimilated quickly to the techniques of this newer and more flexible martial art.

The software and video games for personal computers in Vietnam were all "cracked" versions, bought cheaply on recorded compact discs (CDs). There were streets in downtown Hanoi city that had become specialized in selling personal computers' hardware and software. Using my personal computers, I was exposed to and played many of the classic PC games of that time. As a result, I went to the popular video game rental place in Ngoc Ha village less often. Eventually, I stopped going there permanently after my good friend Trung moved to Germany with his mother, who previously came there as an export worker. Instead, I played a soccer video game on the Sony PlayStation with my university classmates at various other rental places.

Indoctrination and Corruption

At the university, I spent minimal time studying and performed poorly. In many classes, the students just wrote down word by word what the lecturer said and tried to memorize the content. There was only one designated textbook for each class, and the whole curriculum was fixed without any electives or options. The students were also required to take indoctrination classes like Marxist-Leninist Philosophy and Scientific Socialism. The quality control for the student's grades for each class was worse than that of high school because there was only one exam at the end of the semester.

The exam's content for each student was a small portion randomly selected from the body of the textbook. Each student had two tries to obtain a passing score for an exam. Cheating was popular in the form of bringing a microcopy of the textbook into the exam room. Bribery was also common in the university, like in government institutions. It was casual for a student or a group of students to go to a lecturer's home with an envelope of money in exchange for a passing or favorable score on the exam. Influenced by the culture of the time, I also tried cheating and using bribery a couple of times. Nevertheless, I did not feel like that was how I wanted to operate through university.

The relationship among students in my university class was also less sincere and included some spiteful rivalry. There was nothing notable about me, and some students in my class called me '*Tuấn naïve*' because I had no people skills or social understanding. Physically, I was weak, around 1.72 meters tall, and weighed around 50 kilograms, as I used to eat little since childhood. Thus, I had a small stomach and very little stamina. I could easily get sick and was used to receiving treatments with antibiotics since early childhood. One day, I participated in a soccer game with my classmates but puked soon after running for a while, so I quit in humiliation. The dominant and practically only sport that the students played was soccer. My university only had a small concrete playground primarily for basketball, so the students had to rent a small dirt field in a nearby town.

Unusual Connections

In my second year, the secretary of my class's Communist Youth Union Committee was caught taking the recent university entrance exams as an impostor for a hopeful university applicant. Taking university entrance exams for money as an impostor on someone else's behalf was a rising problem nationally. The class secretary got suspended for one year of university attendance as punishment. The whole first year, governing and political personnel of my class got replaced by a different crew of crafty students. They were good at politics and influencing other students in my class and got elected by the class. One of the only two female students in my class also moved to China to study at a university over there. I was somewhat intimidated by the new monitor and secretary of the class as they made known their political alliance and power.

I kept in touch with Thủy, the previously mentioned friend from Yen Hoa High School. He was accepted to Hanoi Medical University and was doing well in his second university year. My childhood friend Hải, on his second-year attempt, got admission to the Architecture Department of the National University of Civil Engineering as one of the top scorers on the entrance exams.

Previously, my aunt and uncle-in-law, who was an officer at the Ministry of Foreign Affairs, traveled to the United States and lived in

New York City for work. They invited my paternal grandmother to visit them for several months. Because of this connection and life experience in the United States, my family members and I had an increased favorable view of the country. It was also during this time that I first watched the newly released American movie '*The Matrix*.' I was completely in awe while watching it, and it was surreal in my mind that such a movie was made and its content was possibly true.

Spiritual Movie

In the movie '*The Matrix,*' there was this guy named Neo, a computer hacker living in the current real world of the movie viewers. Miraculously, a message out of nowhere appeared on his computer screen that called on his name and instructed him to follow a rabbit sign. Subsequently, a crowd appeared in his apartment building, knocking on his apartment door to buy his hacked CD and preach to him about Jesus, which he did not believe in. However, he saw the rabbit sign from the crowd and followed them.

Neo then met a woman with super speed and strength named Trinity, who warned him of the danger after him. Subsequently, Neo was captured by three mysterious agents, who miraculously sealed Neo's mouth and forced a machine-biological bug into his belly button. Trinity and her team contacted Neo and removed the machine-biological bug from his body. Being presented with the choice of believing in what he currently believes or the truth, Neo selected to know what he did not know.

The truth was shown to Neo in his own eyes that a vast number of humans were grown and enclosed in liquid cells to extract their energy through a network of physical machines. People's brains were plugged in with a cord feeding the world they believed in. However, it was a software program called the Matrix to fool them. Neo was unplugged from his cell and physically rescued by Trinity and her team. Neo was shown that the three mysterious agents were computer program entities whose job was to eliminate the truth and keep people believing in the Matrix. Only a few humans knew the truth, but they were continuously hunted down and killed by the agents in the Matrix or by the physical machines outside the Matrix.

Trinity and her team believed Neo was the savior of humans who could defeat the machines controlled by Artificial Intelligence, as revealed by the Oracle in the Matrix. Neo was trained via the software installed into his brain and re-entered the Matrix with the team to receive personal revelation from the Oracle. The growth of Neo's trust in the truth manifested in the growth of his abilities in the Matrix. However, a member did not believe in Neo and betrayed the team in exchange for pleasures offered by the Matrix. The team suffered casualties, and Neo eventually got killed by the agents. Miraculously, Trinity insisted on her faith in Neo and brought him back to life with a kiss. With the certainty of the truth, Neo saw through the digital fabrics of the Matrix, and he became invincible, destroyed the agents, and mastered the Matrix.

Positive Life Changes

Back in my university days, Sơn had stepped outside his family and university circle to learn more about adult life. He showed me places to hang out in the evenings and introduced me to some of his acquaintances. One of them was a very handsome guy who reportedly had children with different girls and wore a cross necklace indicating his religious affiliation. Somehow, he called me three times asking me out, but I felt like it was for religious reasons and declined them all. What actually fascinated me was Sơn's showing off his classical guitar skills. I was hooked, got a decent classical guitar for myself, and started taking lessons from the same teacher who taught Sơn. It was one personal lesson and practice assignment per week, and I loved it. I practiced diligently every day and successfully returned assignments to the teacher every week.

My passion for classical guitar had remarkable positive effects on me. I stopped playing video games and focused entirely on practicing. I also started hanging out at an English club downtown Hanoi where people selected interesting topics and discussed them in English once per week. It was hard because the people in the club had much better English and social knowledge than me. However, I enjoyed the learning and experience. At university, I also began to perform better socially and, particularly in English and computer application classes, with integrity and self-esteem.

During my third year at university, my house underwent a third-story addition, so my paternal grandmother often came to help with cooking. She was the best cook I have ever known, with her extensive knowledge and skills in making traditional Vietnamese cuisine. Because of her plentifully delicious and nutritious meals, I ate a lot more than before. Thus, my weight increased to over 70 kilograms. With increasing physical strength and stamina, I also participated in playing soccer with my university class regularly and started to excel at aerial skills and defending in midfield.

By this time, I had learned all major classical guitar skills and got into full performance pieces. Then, the teacher informed me that I had caught up with Sơn. Subsequently, I quit taking guitar lessons but practiced on my own diligently every day and started to perform at home for friends and even once publicly at the previously mentioned English club. My classmates recognized my transformation. So, they stopped calling me '*Tuấn naïve*' and elected me back to the class Youth Union Committee as a vice-secretary. However, I had a rivalry with the current secretary, who was the soccer team's captain as well.

Academic and Social Progression

In my fourth year at university, my father encouraged me to pursue graduate school abroad in an English-speaking country. From local information, we considered universities in Singapore and the UK. So, I started attending this intensive English training class well-known in Hanoi. The class was one of a kind and specialized in training students to do well on the Test of English as a Foreign Language (TOEFL) required for international students. In this class, I met Hạnh, who was beautiful and feminine in my eyes. She was two years younger than me and studied at Foreign Trade University. I considered her a worthy romance prospect and pursued her, but she kept some distance. One day, I visited her at her home, and she told her mother about me, "*His future is going to Singapore,*" without much excitement in her tone.

The study materials in the specialized English class were hard, especially listening comprehension. There were virtually no English teachers in Hanoi who could speak proper American accents for students to hear. There were several book series with cassette tapes for the TOEFL that the class practiced through for listening, vocabulary, grammar, and reading comprehension. I diligently practiced and did all the English homework. Then diligently practiced my classical guitar skills every day. The reading materials in the TOEFL book series were amazingly informative, covering a wide range of topics that fascinated me. It was the first time period in my life that I was totally passionate about my studies because they had a meaningful purpose and promise of a bright future.

At university, I continued to do better socially and academically. Playing soccer regularly with consistent efforts through the years, I became a prominent member of the class team and well-connected with most players. My strength in computer applications and design skills were also put to good use in design projects as these projects were the emphasis of my fourth and fifth university years.

In the fifth year, my progress continued. There was a soccer tournament for all university classes, and I represented my class as the team captain. My team was good with regular practice over the years. However, the former class secretary, also the former captain, conspired a division among the players against me. Subsequently, the team underperformed and did not go far in the tournament as it could have.

Grandmother's Terminal Illness

During this time, my aunt and uncle-in-law were still working in the U.S. for the Vietnam Ministry of Foreign Affairs, and my paternal grandmother was living at 5 Phan Boi Chau Street by herself and got seriously sick. The air duct of her newly installed air-conditioner was mistakenly plugged into the nearby shared toilet, and her lungs got heavily infected, causing continuous coughing. The air duct was later redirected for fresh air, but the damage had been done to my grandmother for a while, so she had great difficulty breathing.

I no longer had any university classes and started working on my graduation project, using a good laptop my father bought for me. So, I moved in to live with my paternal grandmother. My family also hired female helpers from distant provinces to help with cooking and household chores so that I could focus on the graduation project. My paternal grandmother went on to take antibiotics treatment from several doctors in available hospitals. But after some time, with no signs of improvement, the doctors all concluded her illness was terminal and incurable.

One day, while we were desperate, we saw an advertisement on TV about treatments using natural herbs and leaves originating from imperial China. So, we decided to give it a try.

I gave my grandmother a ride on my motorcycle to the advertised location. The place we went to charged us around 90 USD for packs of herbs and leaves that needed to be boiled and then drunk like tea for one month. My grandmother used her life savings to purchase and drink those herbs. Still, after one month, there was no improvement in her coughing. The first place recommended us to a second place, which charged us around 120 USD for their packs of herbs and leaves. After one month, there was still no improvement in my grandmother's coughing. Then, the second place recommended us to a third place, which charged us 300 USD for their packs of secret herbs and leaves. This time, after drinking, my grandmother threw out phlegm from her lung and noticed an improvement in her coughing. So, she kept purchasing and drinking those packs.

University Graduation

In Vietnam, engineering programs at universities take five years to complete. For the last semester, the students typically need to do a graduation project of real-life size, combining many of the disciplines learned in the last three years. The graduation project was critical in evaluating the quality of the students to be awarded a degree and title of engineer. At my university, 10 was theoretically the highest score a student could get for a class or project. However, in many classes, the highest score was 8 or 9, set by the teacher.

My grade point average for over five years was only 6.64. However, I did an excellent job on my graduation project and it achieved an 8.46 score, and my project advisor kept a small portion of my design as a sample. By the summer of 2003, I graduated from my university and earned a Bachelor of Science degree in Civil Engineering.

Unfortunately, there was a shockingly sad incident. One of my classmates from a distant province was killed the day after graduation.

He was too excited and went out to drink. There, he got into a fight and was stabbed multiple times with a knife. It was rumored that local people perceived him as a bad guy in society and neglected his treatment, contributing to his death. I and some classmates visited him lying in a coffin the last time and donated some money to his family before they transported him back home for the funeral. The story was published in a newspaper and was a national sensation.

Preparation for Studying Abroad

Unusual Connections

To focus on the preparation for applying to graduate schools abroad, I did not take any job after graduation but put all my time into the specialized English class and practicing for the TOEFL test. At the same time, I still maintained my classical guitar skills during breaks and for personal enjoyment. During this time, my father met someone who worked for the Vietnam Institute of Americas Studies and had experience living in many countries abroad. His side business was an advisor for applicants to graduate schools in the United States, and he convinced my father it was viable to do so and best equip me for a bright future. Following his recommendation, I took a TOEFL mockup test to assess my English skills level, and I scored 520, which was encouraging but not sufficient since a minimum score of 550 was required. Also, in addition to the TOEFL test, I needed to take and score sufficiently well on the Graduate Record Exam (GRE) test, which was in English and on another level of difficulty in verbal, quantitative, and analytical writing skills.

Highly motivated by my vision of one day living and studying in the United States, the Promised Land as people said, I kept studying hard for my test and really enjoyed my study material. At this time, there were dial-up internet connections available in Hanoi, and I found some pornography websites that originated from the United States where small video clips could be downloaded. My grandmother's health had improved greatly as she was still taking the secret herbs and leaves. And when my grandmother was not around or at the neighbor's place, I watched pornographic video clips and also showed the female helper, and we had sex.

Foreign Standardized Tests

I took the official TOEFL test at an authorized test center in Hanoi in October 2003 and then immediately put all my efforts into practicing for the GRE test. At that time, the only preparation materials I got were the sample test provided by the test administrator and one Indian preparation software I found and bought via the internet, which was very good in my eyes. However, there was not enough time for me to go through even one round of the preparation software as I took the only official GRE test available of the year in November 2003. After taking the test and realizing the gap between my current skills and what I needed to score high, I continued to practice hard on the materials and even made a copy of the '*GRE: Practicing to Take the General Test: Big Book*' to study. In early 2004, I received my scores on the two tests. On the TOEFL, I got 610 on the multiple-choice sections, which were excellent encompassing listening, grammar, and reading comprehension, and a 4.0 on the writing section, which was decent. On the GRE, I got 440 on verbal and 720 on quantitative skills, which was decent for engineering majors, and 3.5 on analytical writing skills, which was acceptable.

With my required official test scores more than sufficient, the advisor that my father met now persuaded him that he could help me apply to graduate schools in the United States successfully by avoiding known pitfalls and careful preparation of recommendation letters and statements of purpose. My father let me know that he agreed and paid the advisor 4,000 USD for the service. The advisor also recommended that I apply for the Vietnam Education Foundation (VEF) fellowship program, where applicants go through examinations and an interview process, and winners will be supported financially and recommended for graduate study at leading U.S. universities and will be required to return to Vietnam for at least two years after completion of the study.

I applied for the VEF program, and I had to take a general mathematics test and a general physics test administered by VEF. These multiple-choice tests were strange to me as they were in English with mathematics and physics terminologies that I was not familiar with. Nevertheless, I performed relatively well on these tests compared to the applicant pool and was selected for the final round of interviews. The interview was none of what I expected; there were American professors, including a faculty from the University of California at Berkeley and also a member of the United States National Academy of Engineering. I was asked about calculus and differential equations, which I did not know the terminologies of, and my knowledge was rusty. I was also asked about research and any original thesis, which I had no idea about. My strength had been in doing design projects and computer applications rather than mathematics and research. I also had never been formally trained or tested in English speaking skills.

Applying to U.S. Graduate Schools

I was not selected for the VEF fellowship program, and my focus shifted to applying directly to U.S. universities likely within my capability. I heard about and liked New York, where my aunt and uncle-in-law used to live, so I chose Cornell University, Columbia University, The City University of New York, Syracuse University, The State University of New York at Buffalo (SUNY Buffalo), and Texas Tech University where the son of the advisor was studying at. My Bachelor's degree and transcript were translated into English, and the advisor prepared a statement of purpose and three different letters of recommendation with some of my input. The first letter was from my graduation project advisor, who truthfully testified to my excellent performance. The second letter was from the current Dean of Graduate Study at Hanoi Architectural University, who was not my direct teacher but knew about me through Dũng, a socially well-connected younger brother of my paternal grandmother. The Dean highly praised me in the letter to support the plan. The third letter was from one of the Vice Directors of the National Institute of Architecture, testifying for my extra-curricular activities with the Institute, which did not actually happen. Also included in my application was a letter from the Institute of International Education's office in Hanoi to clarify the grading system in Vietnam.

I was very optimistic and thrilled that after years of diligent efforts, I had come close to the near impossibility of studying and living in the United States. Somehow, I still had a very strong longing for Thư, my first crush, and the hope that it would still work out between us. So I contacted her via the phone, hoping she would be persuaded by my bright future. But what I got was a rude awakening; not only did she not care, but she also mockingly told me, "*Enough said, and you still could not understand? Bye-bye!*" My feelings were hurt deeply, and my hope was shattered as I came to realize that was the end of this, and forever so. I only emotionally recovered from it after a while and accepted the fact that my only desirable prospect left was Hạnh.

After completing and sending the applications to the chosen universities with the guidance of the advisor, I continued to work on my English vocabulary for the GRE and improved my classical guitar skills. I also took an additional English writing class and a spoken English class taught by a well-reputed teacher, but it was in British English because there was no qualified spoken American English teacher. I anticipated that I might need to take the GRE test again to obtain competitive enough scores for admissions. At this time, Hạnh and her parents seemed to have a more favorable view of me after knowing about my performance on the difficult tests and my prospect of studying in the United States. Per the request of some friends in the specialized English class, before I quit, I performed some skillful classical guitar pieces at a music café and seemingly captured Hạnh's heart.

By April 2004, I started to get some results from the admission process. I was politely rejected by Columbia University as its letter stated there were not enough seats available to accommodate me. Syracuse University sent me an acceptance letter, and as a private school, its cost for one year of study for international students was estimated to be around $32,000. Then, I got the acceptance letter from SUNY Buffalo. Its corresponding cost as a public school was estimated at only around $20,000, the lowest I found around, and I would receive financial aid as a teaching assistant if I later scored sufficiently high on the Test of Spoken English. I also found out that the Structural Engineering Department at SUNY Buffalo was particularly strong nationally, especially in earthquake engineering. I was accepted to its Master of Science in Structural and Earthquake Engineering program.

Selection of Graduate School

Even though I had not yet received admission results from the remaining schools, I felt like their slow responses were not a good sign. Also, I was happy with the low cost and quality of the program at SUNY Buffalo, so I decided to choose its program early. Following guidance from the advisor, I notified the other schools of my decision and asked SUNY Buffalo to issue Form I-20, Certificate of Eligibility for Nonimmigrant Student Status, so I can apply for an F-1 student visa from Hanoi to travel to Buffalo, New York. According to the advisor and local information, my family also needed to prove sufficient financial resources to support the cost of my study program, and interviewing for the visa was a difficult final hurdle that many people failed by making mistakes.

Following the guidance of the advisor, my parents obtained the necessary financial documents in compliance with American standards, and after receiving Form I-20, I applied for a visa with the U.S. Embassy in Hanoi. I was also advised not to eagerly approach the interviewer, and to answer slowly and clearly. During the interview, I recognized that I was tested for honesty and intention of coming to the United States. I answered honestly about the low scores in my university years and my writing tests, and that I had no family members currently living in the States. I passed the interview with flying colors and obtained the U.S. visa six weeks later, and celebrated the good news with friends and family. At this time, my paternal grandmother had been completely cured of her illness and even grew back her black hair. She stopped taking the secret herbs and leaves as her savings were depleted, but she still cooked me delicious Vietnamese traditional dishes. While waiting for my flight to the U.S., I reviewed my mathematics and engineering knowledge, and also fully memorized Barron's GRE 3000-word list.

I got extremely excited. I recalled my fascinating experience when I first visited the Soviet Union a long time ago. I imagined that I would see streets paved with pure gold like transparent glass in the United States since it was the mythical Promised Land people talked about.

Graduate School Days in Buffalo, New York

New Home and Friends

I left Hanoi, Vietnam, to get on a 30-hour flight that first stopped at Tokyo, Japan, for 10 hours. Then it stopped at the United States port of entry in Chicago, Illinois, for around 3 hours before my final domestic flight to Buffalo, New York, which arrived on the evening of July 27, 2004. Before the flight, I contacted the Vietnamese Graduate Student Association (VGSA) at SUNY Buffalo, and I was welcomed to join and live in a rental property with some existing students. The person who came and received me at the Buffalo airport and gave me a car ride to my new place with him was Đức. He was the Secretary of the VGSA and a second-year Ph.D. student in Computer Science working as a Research Assistant.

I was breath taken and fascinated by the new land's tranquil atmosphere and how different the buildings, streets, and scenery were when compared to that of Hanoi, Vietnam. My new home was a two-story residential dwelling at 371 Lisbon Avenue owned by a Chinese-American landlord, and there was a bedroom in the back available for me. The cost of living in Buffalo was one of the lowest in the country, and my monthly rent was only around $300.

The people living in the house besides Đức were Long, the President of the VGSA and fifth year Ph.D. student in Mathematics working as a Teaching Assistance. Anh and Tường were both second-year graduate students in Computer Science and were winners of the previous and first-generation VEF fellowship program. Dũng was a first-year graduate student like I was, but he majored in Computer Science. Quân was a third-year Ph.D. student in American Studies and a recipient of a Fulbright scholarship. There was only one American student living in the house, but he later moved away.

Within the VGSA, several other Ph.D. students in Mathematics lived in a different house. It was the only house besides mine that VGSA members lived in at that time, and it was not far away. There was also the Vietnamese Student Association at SUNY Buffalo. However, its members were students of Southern Vietnamese descent whose original families fled the country as refugees during the Vietnam War, and they upheld a different national flag. At this time, Hạnh and I loosely established a long-distance relationship as we used a webcam to video chat via Yahoo Messenger.

International Student Life

I had about a month to assimilate into my new life and the university before the fall semester started. My living place was next to the south campus of the university, but the buildings where my classes were conducted were on the north campus. There were regular university bus rides between the south and the north campus. Most of the students, including me, walked almost all the time and everywhere on both campuses. Đức had a car, and he was nice to regularly give housemates rides to grocery stores and sometimes to other places that were far away.

I remember one day while riding with Đức. I saw an African-American kid on a bicycle who looked at us and shouted, "*Chinese trash!*" I was shocked, but Đức told me, "*The high crime and violence areas are neighborhoods where black people live.*" I had heard about racial discrimination, and what Đức said sounded like a racial bias, but later, I came to know that it was statistically correct.

Another day, while I was at home, there was a knock on the door. When I opened the door, there was a middle-aged Caucasian woman showing me a picture of beautiful scenery with peaceful children, a lion, and other animals together. She asked if I knew about God, but I answered that I believe in science, not religion, and closed the door on her.

I was intimidated and proud at the same time as a student in the Structural and Earthquake Engineering graduate program at SUNY Buffalo. The program housed the National Center for Earthquake Engineering Research, created by the National Science Foundation in 1986 and then renamed the Multidisciplinary Center for Earthquake Engineering Research (MCEER) in 1998.

The faculties of the program were doing cutting-edge research that was published in top peer-reviewed journals and incorporated into the latest structural building codes. Many students in the program and my class were Chinese who completed their Master's degree in China and were already familiar with the technical knowledge. There were only a couple of American students, and I was the only Vietnamese in the program, so everything was like a puzzle to me.

Academic Struggles

From the Department policy, I found out that a minimum score of 55 on the SPEAK test was required for all international graduate assistants before the semester began. I registered for the test and practiced hard within the two weeks available but only scored 40. The test result reflected that I had minimal English-speaking skills, particularly with the North American accent.

For the first semester, I registered for some required foundational courses for my program. Also, I took the Advanced Spoken English class to improve my speaking skills. The foundational courses were very hard for me as they were highly advanced compared to what I knew and covered a lot of materials. What also struck me hard was my difficulty understanding what the professors stated in classes as they talked in different accents, using many terminologies unknown to me.

At home, I also did not understand what people said on television as they spoke fast using casual language. Even though I did well on the listening comprehension of the TOEFL test, in reality, people did not speak perfect English with clarity. Nevertheless, I enjoyed the experience and learning new technical knowledge, and I tried and focused as hard as I could. Every day, including weekends, I cooked food and stuffed it into plastic containers to carry them to the north campus for study and returned home late in the evening.

During the semester break, Long, Đức, Anh, Tường, and I made a weekend road trip to visit New York City, and it was a memorable and good time for us. We visited the Statue of Liberty, the iconic symbol of America I had seen on television since childhood. I understood the value of liberty but was unable to comprehend why the symbol was a god and a female.

At the end of the semester, I was awfully disappointed with my grade as I barely maintained the minimum 3.0 Grade Point Average (GPA). I got an A, the highest possible grade equal to a 4.0 GPA, in the Advanced Spoken English class because it was much easier. But that did not count in my GPA for the program. I realized the internationally competitive nature of the program I was in and that many students in my class were first in their home university.

And I was shown to be near the bottom in academic performance. I also found out that teaching assistantship was only for first-year graduate students, and from the second year forward, a student seeking financial aid needs to find a research assistantship from one of the professors. I talked to some professors in the program, and they all seemed to require excellent grades, at least an A in their class. My housemates, Long and Đức, were doing excellent as straight-A students, and others in the house were also doing fine.

Unusual Connections

I was excited about my first winter abroad. Seeing and playing with snow for the first time was magical. It was chilly and snowy in Buffalo since the city was right next to the Great Lake Erie, which caused additional lake-effect snow. Also, there was an issue with the heating system of my room, which was yet to be fixed. So, I had to wear warm clothes with a hat and sleep inside a sleeping bag rated at -30 degrees Fahrenheit.

The winter break provided me with the time I extremely needed to learn about other things outside of university life. I learned how to use eBay and Amazon websites and explored the internet for information on just about anything. Along with a television show we were watching, Long noted the housemates of String Theory, a promising candidate for the theory of everything based on pure mathematics. I realized that in the U.S., there were many resources, many differing activities, opinions, viewpoints, and a vast possibility for what a person can achieve that fascinated my imagination.

Out of my curiosity and thirst for knowledge, I started to search and purchase a variety of books from Amazon other than my required textbooks. Some were supplements for my engineering program, and others were related to social success like '*How to Win Friends and*

Influence People,' '*Dressing Smart for Men,'* and then '*The Lay Guide: How to Seduce Women More Beautiful Than You Ever Dreamed Possible No Matter What You Look Like or How Much You Make*' in which the contents impressed me as much as the title did.

That book convinced me of the advertised success as its knowledge and methods were extensively tested and practiced over the years by a number of successful pickup artists. I put what I learned to work by confidently approaching and talking to random American girls I met on campus. And indeed, I got certain positive feedback, which was refreshing. This reinforced in my mind a near-term life goal of being successful with women, even the trophy American girls considered out of my league.

Also, during the winter break, my housemates and I were invited to dinner at an American home. The family was Christian and volunteered to build relationships with international students at our university. The husband was Don, the wife was Ruth, and they had several kids. The idea that they were Christian seemed not a good fit for us, who all believed in science, but we figured other than their religious view, which was a cultural thing, they were genuinely nice to us.

Their house was in a rural area far from the university campus, where they home-schooled their kids and had homegrown foods. Not everyone in the house went, but Long, Đức, Anh, and I; and we had a great time. It was strange that Don and Ruth prayed before the meal, and we all submitted to the prayer as a polite thing to do. Their homemade American food was amazingly delicious, and the pie was the best I ever had. We also had interesting conversations about life in America, what their family was doing and planned to do, and even about science and its fascinating theories.

Ups and Downs of Student Life

At the beginning of the second semester, Bing, a Chinese and Ph.D. student in my class whom I sometimes learned from, warned me of the Advanced Steel Structures course by Professor Bruneau, director of MCEER. Bing said his course was extremely heavy, and even an excellent female Ph.D. student of the previous year only got a B from the professor. His class started at 7 AM twice a week when it was still dark and covered from undergraduate materials to current cutting-edge research and design, along with extensive homework more than any other course. Only an engineer who practiced both in Vietnam and the U.S. would understand the stark differences in design practice.

Steel structural design in the U.S. was extensively coded in a few thousand pages code book and updated regularly called the Steel Construction Manual using Imperial units and incorporated many factors, failure modes, and material limit states. In contrast, steel structural design in Vietnam using Metric units was primitive, mostly based on the strength of materials within elastic limits. I quickly fell behind in the course but still learned as much as possible about all the new technical knowledge and design practices.

The Advanced Spoken English class recommended that I register for practice sessions with an American student. At the registration table, I met Krystal, a talkative blonde and a graduate student studying Spanish. I dressed well and acted cool. Still, unexpectedly, she touched my arm and said that I had tan skin and invited me to her church meeting in a few days, to which I agreed.

Later, as previously arranged, I was picked up in a car by Krystal and her sister Brittany, going to their church not far from campus. Brittany was two years younger than her sister and extremely attractive in my eyes as she epitomized the American trophy girl. I dressed my best and acted confidently, and unexpectedly, Krystal said to Brittany, "*If he proposes, I will agree.*" They both flirted with me.

Their church was a big gathering of many young people, and I had a great time and was playful. At the end of the night, we all really liked each other, and they drove me back to my place, and Krystal hugged me goodbye. I met them a few more times after that and briefly dated a few other girls on campus. But all these relationships did not progress any further.

In winter, the university campuses were covered in very thick snow, except for the walkways, which were plowed often. Buffalo frequently had snow storms and was infamous for having people die in cars covered in snow. Every time I went to class and back home, I walked across a big snow field on the south campus for a shortcut, and sometimes I slipped and fell on the slippery sidewalks in the neighborhood.

Near the end of the semester, I got sick. I repeatedly coughed and felt dizzy. So, I went for a health examination at the medical center on campus that accepted my medical insurance for international students. The medical examiner noticed a white area inside one of my ears and thought it was a Q-tip. So, she tried to take it out, but it did not work. Later, the examiner discovered it was an ear infection and declared me allergic to spring pollen, which had never happened to me in Vietnam. I took the prescription pills, but they did not help much.

I performed poorly in the final exam and got a C+ in the Advanced Steel Structures course. I talked to Professor Bruneau after receiving my grade, expressing my intention to repeat the course. But, he commented that I did not need to make an impression; if I repeated the course, the new grade would not replace my initial grade. Bing was one of three students who got an A. He was awarded a Research Assistantship by

Professor Bruneau and immediately started working under his supervision.

Luckily, I got an A- in Earthquake Engineering and Foundation Dynamics, a less competitive course, and maintained my overall minimum required GPA. My roommate Tường, who had completed his Master's on a J-1 visa at the end of the semester and was required to return to Vietnam, suggested a celebration. So, I treated my housemates to a seafood buffet in a casino in Niagara Falls, and we had a blast eating a lot of snow crab legs.

Some Life Lessons

After the first school year, a graduate student's future in my department was mostly determined. Competitive students who performed well found professors with funding to work with via Research Assistantship. Underperformed students were kicked out of the program, and less competitive students started looking for a job in the civil engineering industry if possible. Some were successful in their job search even before or without getting a degree. I also heard from some students in the program that some professors had available funding but kept it for themselves instead.

For international students who wish to stay in the U.S., finding a job in the States is vital. Therefore, I decided to do a project for my Master's degree during the summer, so that I could have time to prepare for my job search later.

Professor Filiatrault, deputy director of MCEER, accepted me to participate in one of his current projects where I could use my computer applications skills. In that seismic analysis project, I built a finite-element model and a mathematical model of steel storage racks and derived their dynamic responses to ground motions of the 1994

Northridge earthquake. By the end of the summer, I completed my project portion successfully without much difficulty.

There were also other things going on during the summer. I took a day bus trip organized by the university for students to travel to Toronto, Canada. And there, we visited the CN Tower and its glass floor.

Back in Buffalo, my housemates were entertained by my new attitude that life is short and a winning male shall score with multiple attractive girls. The exception was Quân, who insisted that what matters is when you die. His response baffled everyone, but he did not explain why.

Later, some housemates and I went to a famous yearly festival in Buffalo called Canal Fest of the Tonawandas. It was a blast; that was the first time I saw policemen riding horses. Accidentally, I met Krystal along the way and saw some people promoting Scientology, which I had seen on campus. It was the first time we talked about our beliefs. We both did not believe in Scientology as I did some reading about it, and I claimed truth in science. What struck me was Krystal's response, "*God created science.*" It was logically sound, but nobody had ever told me that before.

At home, I searched and read online about ways to obtain wealth, financial freedom, and the Law of Attraction. And seemingly a coincidence via an email out of nowhere, I was contacted by a self-proclaimed attorney looking for a next of kin to inherit 7,900,000 USD from a deceased American citizen named Adam Tran. He sent me various documentation with unfamiliar certifications, but they looked legitimate.

He even called me over the phone, and I was convinced this was the fortune resulting from the Law of Attraction. I sent him 600 USD via Western Union to cover the required administrative cost. However, in the next step, he asked for 3,200 USD to continue the process, and that was when I realized it was a scam. That was the first time I was scammed in America.

Looking for Jobs

I started looking for jobs during the third semester of my engineering program while taking the remaining required courses and credits for the degree. It was another learning experience for me. I searched online on engineering job boards across the United States and in local ads. I attended a career fair and consultation offered by the university. I learned that I needed a pertinent resume and cover letter tailored for each job I wanted to apply for. Also, I had to take and pass the 8-hour Fundamental of Engineering (FE) exam to be competitive in my application, which was also required to earn a professional engineer license in the future.

As an international student with an F-1 visa, I also needed to apply for Optional Practical Training (OPT), which allowed me to work in the U.S. for one year within the field of my degree program. Finding an entry-level job that I would be qualified for was hard since I had no work experience in the U.S. But, I applied to all suitable openings I found online. After a while, I got some phone interviews. I even paid for a domestic flight for an in-person interview for a job near New York City. I did not get an offer, but I gained some experience.

My job search activities negatively affected my performance in the courses I took that semester. I did fine in the Advanced Concrete Structures course and got a B+. However, in the Finite Element Analysis course, I fell behind after a while, and the textbook referred by the professor did nothing to teach the fundamentals but was a collection of research papers on the subject.

Even worse, the professor forgot to provide the shape function required to solve the first problem with subsequent questions in the final exam.

Only after the exam, I recalled the professor adding the missing information on the blackboard during exam time when I was extremely focused and struggling to figure out the problem. In the end, one student in the class got an F and was dismissed academically from the program. I did not fail but got a B- in the course.

In the Bridge Engineering course, there was homework to replicate engineering codes. After understanding it, I copied the homework file from a classmate with various typos as mine. The course instructor found out our homework was alike. I admitted my wrongdoing, resubmitted the corrected homework, and accepted half the credits as a penalty. Also, in this course, we had to do the final project in a group of two. Unfortunately, my assigned partner had to undergo a surgery and could no longer help halfway through. I could not finish the project single-handedly before the deadline and got a B- in the course.

While I had earned enough credits for my Master's program, my GPA fell just below 3.0, putting me on probationary status and the risk of not getting my degree. Therefore, I talked to Professor Weber, the Department Chair, about my situation, and he accepted my petition to do additional work for a grade change in the Bridge Engineering course. Despite initial discouragement from some classmates and Professor Bruneau, I also decided to retake the Advanced Steel Structures for my final semester.

The Breakthroughs

By taking only one course in the final semester, I could review the important materials I learned throughout my engineering program. I put in as much time as I wish to focus on what matters and master the knowledge and problem-solving skills tested on the exams.

An area not well developed but important in the Advanced Steel Structures course was the collapse mechanism analysis of structures.

The currently known solution was a trial-and-error method of calculating different assumed collapse mechanisms and then back-tested until finding the correct one. In the textbook used for the course, there was a presentation about tabulating basic collapse mechanisms and combining them case by case to help find the solution because it was not possible to combine them systematically.

Digging deeper than what the textbook presented via my own analysis, I found a way to dissect basic collapse mechanisms in more detail and assign them uniformity of convention so they could be combined systematically. I used this method in the midterm exam to get the correct answer and scored 91 out of 100. Professor Bruneau commented on the method I used in the midterm exam, "*Not really, but I will accept.*" I came to discuss it with him, and he said he was pleased with my performance. Ultimately, he added two more points to my midterm score for a 93.

During this time, I registered for the FE exam with the state of New York scheduled for October 2006, applied for OPT which was expected to be approved in a few months, attended a driving course and obtained my New York driving license. I also continued reviewing my engineering knowledge, paid for a company online to compose my resume and cover letter, and applied for all the suitable jobs I found.

As a result, I got more phone interviews, and M.A. Engineering Inc., in Las Vegas, Nevada, paid me to fly over for an in-person interview. The firm was doing structural design for several high-rise buildings and casinos nationwide, and their five engineers asked me technical questions non-stop. I confidently and successfully answered them all. After the interview, the female office manager asked if I did well and commented, "*The job is extremely boring!*"

Back in Buffalo, I also got an in-person interview with a local company but was asked only a few technical questions. Only one week after the interview, M.A. Engineering Inc. offered me a job starting at $20 an hour and asked me to respond quickly with the promise of sponsoring a work visa H-1B in the future. I liked what the firm was doing and the allure of life in Las Vegas, so I accepted immediately. The local company in Buffalo also offered me a job later, but I was already preparing to move to Las Vegas at the end of the semester.

New Understandings

I continued to improve my method of systematically analyzing and combining collapse mechanisms and used it again in the final exam of the Advanced Steel Structures course. I solved all other problems without difficulty, but the collapse mechanism problem in the final exam was more complex and trickier.

However, my method still robustly worked despite having a big table of parameters, and I turned in a final exam just shy of perfection. I was not surprised when later I received the only grade A I ever got in the whole program. I went to talk to Professor Bruneau. He was impressed with my performance but disappointed that I was moving to work in Las Vegas. My grade in the Bridge Engineering course was also changed to B, so my overall GPA came in at 3.1, and I had completed all requirements for my Master's degree.

It seemed like there was a catalyst and coincidence between the peak of my intellectual capacity in my mid-twenties and my exposure to a vast amount of new information and ideas available in the U.S. By the early summer of 2006 in Buffalo, I had bought and read through a good number of books like '*The Art of War,*' '*The Selfish Gene,*' '*How to be a Billionaire,*' '*The Elegant Universe,*' '*Relativity: The Special and General Theory,*' '*The One Hundred: A Ranking of History's Most Influential Persons.*'

All of the reading connected in my mind into a seemingly solid understanding of human nature and the whole world. It convinced me that there was no free will and each person's life was predetermined, that consciousness of the present time was only relative to each person as the universe has no beginning and no end. My housemates who listened to my arguments and the above conclusions were really impressed.

During this time, I also gained a better understanding of the nature of mathematics by talking with Long and then Tuấn, a recent housemate with the same name as mine who came as a first-year Ph.D. student in Mathematics.

Long asserted the true nature of mathematics was logic but acknowledged that logic only works within its axiomatic system. Tuấn was the first person I heard declaring mathematics was an art, not science, but it was used for science. I realized that anyone could define an arbitrary but specific axiomatic system and then discover all the mathematical results within it. It was akin to creating a new board game with specific rules and exploring what could happen.

Working and Living in Las Vegas, Nevada

Working Life and Challenges

I left Buffalo, New York, to come to Las Vegas, Nevada, near the end of June 2006 to start working for M.A. Engineering Inc. The company paid for my one-week stay in The New Frontier Hotel and Casino on the Las Vegas Strip so I could find a permanent living place in the meantime. I had not yet received my OPT, but it was expected to arrive soon, and I was assigned to work as a structural engineering intern under the supervision of the senior structural engineer, who people called Junior.

It was my first ever job, so at the beginning, I just spent time being familiar with technical documents and computer programs the firm used. I was extremely excited and optimistic about my new life in one of a kind city in the world. I never had a car and needed one to go to work, so I bought without hesitation from CarMax my dream and first car ever, a 2000 Toyota Celica GTS, at a 12% interest rate along with a very high insurance premium. I also found and signed a one-bedroom apartment lease at 3550 Paradise Road, right behind the Las Vegas Strip.

Subsequently, I received my OPT, which expires by the end of June 2007. I couldn't continue to work after my OPT expiration and had a 60-day grace period to either leave the U.S. or change my status to something that legally allowed me to stay. The typical and most common route for an international student to continue working in the U.S. was to be sponsored by an employer for a work visa H-1B up to 3-year duration, then up to another 3-year extension. After that, the employee must either leave the U.S. for at least one year before obtaining another H-1B visa or be sponsored for a Green Card (a Permanent Resident status). These were notorious for their difficulty due to complex administrative and qualification processes and competition from many applicants for a limited number of visas set by Congress. From my findings, many people waited for 10 to 20 years before obtaining Permanent Resident status if they ever got there.

Even though I felt total freedom living alone, it was also depressing compared to living with housemates, where I had people to talk to. I enjoyed my time at work as I started reviewing shop drawings of a high-rise casino, and Junior was a very nice mentor. To save much time from grocery shopping, cooking, and cleaning up, I bought and ate MET-Rx Big 100 Colossal Protein Bars to replace all my meals except when I eat out. I believed they were healthy and nutritious as advertised. At home, I studied hard for my upcoming FE exam, which covered all major engineering disciplines in the morning section and focused on Civil engineering in the afternoon section. The difficulty was in other engineering disciplines that I had to learn. On the good side, it was convenient that I lived close and could spend some evenings checking out the casinos and entertainment spots along the Las Vegas Strip. Around this time, my mother informed me via Yahoo messenger that my first crush, Thu, had married her boyfriend in Vietnam.

Unexpected Job Change

One day at work near the end of August 2006, I saw the owner of M.A. Engineering hastily asked all the engineers to attend a meeting. Junior told me to come in with a chair, and I did so. However, the owner said that the meeting was not for me and asked me to leave them alone, and I did so. I was new and ignorant of the company's operation and real life. I did not understand what was happening. But the same week, on Friday, the office manager called Junior and me into a meeting and said she did not want to do this, but I was fired effective immediately. She informed me that I would get severance pay for two weeks and showed me a list of local civil engineering firms. I couldn't believe what I heard, and inside, I felt like being knocked out permanently by Mike Tyson, but outwardly, I remained calm and left in shock.

At home, I felt like a total defeat, and my world was turned upside down. Worse than not finding a job, besides the apartment lease and furniture rent, I also had a car loan of around $15,000 and all the high maintenance costs. I sent my resume to all the firms in the list I was given and applied to all others I found online. Desperate, I contacted the company that offered me a job back in Buffalo, New York, expressing my willingness to move back, and I was informed that they would need to find out what happened to my previous employment. Luckily, I got interviews from a few local recruiters, leading to some interviews with their clients, and I felt less worried. I also got interviews directly from some of the companies on the list. The last one who responded to my application was G.C. Wallace Inc., one of the largest multi-disciplinary engineering firms headquartered in Las Vegas.

By the time I went to the interview with G.C. Wallace Inc. I already got two job offers from previous interviews at the equivalent of $43,000 and $45,000 salary, so I felt confident and had leverage. Brian, the structural engineering department manager, and Pascal, the vice president and one of the lead structural engineers, interviewed me. I was professional and honest about my current situation, and the interview went well. I was impressed with both Brian's and Pascal's professionalism. I remembered Pascal's comment referring to me, "*You can be the President,*" which I did not expect nor understand why he said such a high word for me. Only after a few days, Brian called me to offer the engineering intern job at $25 an hour and an acknowledgment that I would need sponsorship for a work visa H-1B later, and I accepted immediately with joy. The company in Buffalo also called me back shortly after and reiterated the original offer with the promise to sponsor my work visa H-1B, but I politely declined.

Figuring Out Work and Life

I worked under the supervision of Pascal, and we got along very well, like having a spark. I quickly learned everything and became very productive in my job. It was also strange that during a picnic event very early in my job, one of the structural drafters said he heard I was an extraordinary engineer. I was unsure of the intended meaning then, and he explained it meant I was good. I wondered how that could be known when I was just fresh out of school. At home, I continued studying hard for the FE Civil exam and sometimes went out on the Las Vegas Strip. I got connected with some guys in the local society of pickup artists to learn from and practice how to get the girls in the clubs. It was a fun and eye-opening experience, but the club atmosphere was also extremely noisy and superficial. Most people were visitors who came and went after a short stay, and the guys I went out with never went again.

One day at work, I felt dizzy and had to take sick leave. Also, my nose frequently bled for no clear reason. I went to a doctor using my company's insurance and was told I had an ear infection and a crooked internal nose requiring expensive surgery. I talked to one of my co-workers and was advised to get a second opinion. I searched online and went to a different doctor and was recommended to use simple salt water nose drops without any need for surgery, I did so, and it worked. Another day, I got hurt by an ingrown toenail and went to a doctor. He performed surgery to cut the nail but also accidentally cut away a small portion of my toe and had to put a bandage around it. Overall, I was not impressed with the doctors who recommended expensive surgery procedures while there were other simple and effective treatments available.

I originally registered for the FE exam with New York State, so my exam was proctored when I took it in October 2006 in a testing location in Las Vegas. I did well on the exam, got a passing result on my first attempt, and then applied for and obtained my Engineer In Training (EIT) certificate from the State of Nevada. Subsequently, Brian and Pascal informed me to register and take the 8-hour Principles and Practice of Engineering (PE) exam in October 2007, as the State of Nevada allowed an EIT to do so before obtaining the required work experience to become a licensed engineer. So, I registered for the exam and started studying for it after work. I continued to do well and was very productive on my job and was entrusted by Pascal to make improvements in design template drawings and calculation Excel worksheets.

During this time, big land developers in the Las Vegas metropolitan area bought land and built homes for sale. The need to construct public underground infrastructures, roadways, and bridges came with these.

G.C. Wallace Inc. was serving these developers as clients, and I got involved in structural designs of retaining walls, underground junction structures, pedestrian bridges, and miscellaneous structures. There were technical challenges for some unique situations, but I succeeded in solving them all using advanced structural theories, custom design solutions, and computer applications. Some of my solutions also showed clear savings in construction costs. As a result, I earned more trust and praise from Pascal and Brian.

It was interesting that during this time, one of my married male co-workers told me to talk to a single female around my age on the same work floor but in a different engineering department. However, she was not attractive in my eyes. In the past, I once asked her in a friendly manner to hang out on the Las Vegas Strip, but she declined.

Another interesting thing was during a large meeting for the whole company. The CEO commented that right in front of him were some 300 engineers who were meant to be revered by society. However, the CEO's attitude clearly indicated the engineers, even though mass in number, were insignificant and were just like sheep to be led by him.

Difficulty with Sponsorship

My OPT was going to expire soon, and my request for sponsorship of a work visa H-1B to continue working for the company was supported by Brian. Still, this decision was delayed by upper management. I searched online and came to talk to a local lawyer specializing in H-1B visas. But, he asked me to make an initial payment of around $2000 to start the application immediately or lose out on the limited chance and time window. I informed Brian, and subsequently, multiple management meetings occurred regarding my situation, followed by a pay raise to $27 an hour, but again, a decision still needed to be made. The lawyer's office did not even communicate with me but only contacted Brian regarding the matter. Eventually, the time window for the H-1B application expired without any action from upper management. I felt extremely stressed, working while knowing that my employment would end soon and I would have to leave the U.S. and likely never return.

I searched online for a solution and discovered that with an advanced degree and coming from Vietnam, a country with significantly fewer applicants than China or India, I could be sponsored by my employer directly for a Green Card via the second preference EB-2 category. Then, an immigrant visa would be immediately available for me if everything worked out. However, the application process was even more strict and complex than that of the work visa H-1B. I talked to Brian about this solution, and after he met with upper management, I was encouraged to find a lawyer to help with the process. I contacted M.A. Engineering Inc. for advice since they had experience sponsoring Green Cards for their engineers. I was recommended to a prominent immigration lawyer within the Las Vegas metro area. At first, I balked at the initial fee of $5,000, but after realizing that I needed the lawyer to have a chance of success, I agreed to a total fee of $7,500, which would be paid $500 monthly over 15 months. My company also provided $4,000 to help me with the application.

Surprisingly, the large monetary cost of my Green Card application was not the most difficult part of the process. My application required my employer to provide a detailed job description with the necessary qualifications and advertise it publicly for several months to Americans and permanent residents at a prevailing wage determined by the U.S. Department of Labor. Any qualified American or permanent resident who applied for the job would need to be interviewed and given priority by my employer. After processing provided information, the Department of Labor set a prevailing wage at $32.58 an hour, much higher than the prevailing wage for an H-1B visa and my current pay rate. It caused a delay in the decision from upper management regarding my application again.

Maintaining Legal Status

On my very last working day on OPT, near the end of June 2007, there was still no decision to proceed with my application with the prevailing wage. I hopelessly came to Brian to say goodbye and prepared to leave the U.S. Then Brian called an executive into his office with me and said that I was worth the prevailing wage and that if I had to go, there was nothing personal. When Brian mentioned that I was going to take and would likely pass the PE exam in October 2007, the executive said that the company could pay the prevailing wage for an engineer with a Professional Engineer (P.E.) qualification and allowed my application to proceed to the next step. Going home, I felt much relieved from the several stressful months. However, there were other challenges ahead. I could only legally stay in the U.S. for 60 days after my OPT expiration. I needed to take the PE exam in four months in the future and pass it. I could not work and had no income, yet I had to pay rent, food, utility, car payments, and monthly lawyer fee. Even though hanging out in casinos, I did not gamble any of my savings and had accumulated enough to pay all ongoing expenses for six months.

I put all my time and effort into studying for the PE Civil exam at home. It covered all major areas of civil engineering in the morning section and focused on structural engineering in the afternoon section. But in contrast to the FE exam, the difficulty was in real-world applications and work experience in areas of civil engineering other than structural that I had to learn. By August 2007, I was informed by the lawyer's office that because my application for Labor Certification with the Department of Labor had begun, I was allowed to stay in the U.S. past my OPT grace period to wait for the result.

However, my Nevada driver's license expiration date was based on my OPT status and expired. I could no longer drive nor had a document to show my status in the U.S. There were many crimes surrounding the rental apartments in Las Vegas. I bought a bicycle to move around, but it was stolen shortly after. Another day, the entire laundry load of my new clothes was stolen. My car's glass was shattered at night, and the new GPS device was stolen. Eggs were thrown on my car's windshield, and all the tires were punctured flat. I took buses to get around sometimes, kept ordering online and ate MET-Rx Big 100 Colossal Protein Bars to replace all my meals. In October 2007 I took the PE exam, did well, and felt confident that I would pass on my first attempt. I also moved to a nearby studio apartment at 500 East Sierra Vista Drive to reduce living expenses.

The Breakthrough

Most of the labor forces in Las Vegas were in the hotel and casino service industry. The city had a low concentration of highly educated professionals compared to an average American city. It was an advantage for my Labor Certification application since after advertising the job in a local newspaper, and within the company, for several months, no qualified local American or Green Card holder applied for the job. The U.S. Department of Labor approved my case, and there was an immigration visa immediately available for me from the United States Citizenship and Immigration Services. My immigration application proceeded to the Adjustment of Status stage, where I could apply for a temporary work permit while waiting for the official Green Card. During this waiting time, without any identification document, I stayed home and replayed some of my favorite video games since childhood. By January 2008, I got the temporary work permit card in the mail and immediately went to work the next day. At that time, I had exhausted all my savings and just started to have a negative balance in my bank account.

I resumed working for G.C. Wallace Inc., this time as an Engineering Intern II at the same pay rate as before, and at the same time I also got a passing result for my PE exam. However, the Nevada Board of Professional Engineers only gave two years of education credits for my five-year Bachelor's degree. Therefore, I needed six years of work experience to become a licensed engineer in Nevada. The company would need to pay me at the prevailing wage according to the law when I officially receive my Green Card to become a permanent U.S. resident. No more land development projects were going on at this time, and I was assigned to work on the Las Vegas Convention Center Enhancement Project. It was a public project where several engineering and architectural companies worked together in a joint office under the umbrella of HNTB Corporation. During this time, I always dressed and looked my best, and it was again interesting that the female office manager, whom I did not know, told me to talk to a single female around my age on the same work floor but from a different company. However, I neither knew her nor appreciated why I should go to her if she was interested.

Back home in Vietnam, my parents officially divorced, and my father informed me of the decision. My father said he did not want me to be emotionally affected and kept the marriage as long as possible, but my mother stubbornly requested the divorce. I was not emotionally affected as I never saw a deep loving connection between my parents and I had no attachment to it. I was glad my parents were released from what made them unhappy, and my father was free to live with the woman at his workplace who knew how to care for him. Also, after a long time out of no contact, Hạnh let me know via Yahoo Messenger that she met her fiancé, an international student from Vietnam, while doing her graduate study in Sweden. She commented that originally, she did not truly like me, implying what attracted her was only my perceived bright future. I congratulated her, and that was the last time we communicated. It was me who changed my mind first to pursue an American trophy girl instead of her.

U.S. Permanent Residency

April 30, 2008, was the day that I officially became a U.S. permanent resident, as shown on the Green Card I received in the mail. I reported my new status to my company, and there was no increase in my pay rate to the set prevailing wage. Then, after consulting with the immigration lawyer, my company started to pay me $32.6 per hour, including retrospective payment to my original date of new status. As a permanent resident, I had all the rights of a U.S. citizen except the right to vote. Also, to maintain permanent resident status, I must physically live in the U.S. for the majority of the calendar year and shall not commit any crime. After five years of maintaining permanent resident status, I could apply for U.S. citizenship. I informed some of my housemates, still living and studying in Buffalo, New York, about my new status, and they were amazed.

After consulting with Brian, and since the company had an office in California and the California Board for Professional Engineers gave full educational credits for my Bachelor's and Master's degrees, I registered for the 5-hour California Civil Examinations in April 2009, which consisted of two separate exams: the Seismic Principles exam and the Engineering Surveying exam.

During this time, by reading about the history of mathematics, I discovered a century-old fact with profound philosophical implications. David Hilbert, one of the most influential 19th and early 20th-century mathematicians, started a research project known as Hilbert's Program to formulate all mathematics on a consistent and complete logical foundation. However, his attempt was proven futile by the work of Kurt Gödel, one of the most significant logicians in history. Gödel's

Incompleteness theorems proved that any set of axioms you could posit as a possible foundation for mathematics would inevitably be incomplete: there will always be statements about natural numbers that are true but unprovable, and no candidate set of axioms can ever prove its own consistency. It meant there could be no mathematical theory of everything or unification of what's provable and true. Also, Gödel's proofs for the two theorems were so novel in the approach that a layperson with middle school math skills could understand.

It was indeed a milestone success in life for me to legally immigrate to the U.S. after 3.5 years of my first arrival as an international student. Then, having a professional job with a comfortable income, I felt greater than ever. The only thing I felt missing was a trophy American girlfriend. I resumed hanging out at bars and nightclubs on the Las Vegas Strip and met attractive girls who were '*working*' girls, as they called themselves. I did not go with them initially but eventually gave in and used the so-called '*escort service*' from a local advertisement, a cover-up for prostitution, a few times. Ultimately, it cost serious money, and deep down, I did not feel fulfilled. I longed for a deep and lasting connection with someone beautiful in appearance but also a faithful and loving partner.

Dabbling in the Stock Market

No longer studying for any professional exam in the near term, I purchased and read various books from Amazon about business, financial markets, investments, and trading. By the fall of 2008, I registered for an evening class in Microeconomics at the University of Nevada, Las Vegas (UNLV) as a non-degree student to formally study the subject after work. I did well and got a grade A in the end, but I noticed the instructor verbally claimed a Ph.D. degree, but on the university's website, it showed he had only a Master's degree.

The bust of the housing bubbles, the collapse of the financial markets, and the election of President Barack Obama dominated the end of 2008. Like what was happening all over the country, my company was downsizing and laying off many people, including engineers who were supposed to be revered by society and treasured by management. Pascal had also left the company, but I kept working on the Las Vegas Convention Center Enhancement Project.

Recognizing the rare opportunity of an extreme downturn in the financial markets, using my own $15,000 savings and $10,000 given by my father, I opened my first-ever brokerage account with Firstrade Securities and explored different investment options. Influenced by what I learned about trading and noticing the daily trend in the U.S. stock market, I started day trading different stocks using leverage and short-selling and learned how to make quick profits. I was still working full-time, but the work had already slowed down a lot, and I managed to enter the trading position early and closed it at the end of the trading hours. My strategy worked well, as during this time the U.S. stocks were very volatile, and many trended in a single direction during the day, up or down. So, my brokerage account ballooned to around $75,000 over two months.

The Great Recession

By early 2009, it was clear that the country was in a Great Recession, and Las Vegas, the center of the housing bubble, got hit the hardest. The city of Las Vegas stopped funding indefinitely for its projects, and I was reassigned to work on the finishing phase of the McCarran International Airport's Terminal 3 Roadways project. My company kept laying off more people and closed all the offices except one where everyone still with the company was gathered together. One strange thing I noticed about Drew, one of the drafters in my engineering department, was that he once vehemently told me to get away from his face because I was somewhat sick but later said he loved me as his neighbor, which I believed to be genuine. This time, Drew corrected some shop drawings for a contractor. Every time it came back exactly the same despite his careful and specific instructions, and it frustrated him. Then, subsequently, he got laid off.

To prepare for uncertainty and cut down living expenses, I moved to a shared living in a townhouse at 1450 Hialeah Drive with the owner and another tenant and paid monthly rent. Even though restricted in space and what I could do, I had housemates to talk with, and we had a good connection. I also started studying for the California Civil Exams and took another evening class in Macroeconomics at UNLV. In this class, I learned the Invisible Hand concept, introduced by Adam Smith, which says that by letting individuals act in their self-interests in a free market economy, the best interest of society is fulfilled.

Metaphorically, according to Smith, divine providence is the hand of God that works to make this happen. Interestingly, this was akin to a religious belief in something that did not exist. The ongoing financial crisis and the government's bailing out of banks too big to fail provided evidence to the contrary of the concept.

My hours were cut down more at work, and I was assigned to work only two days a week. Realizing it would be this bad or worse in Las Vegas for a long time, I asked Brian to lay me off. It was in April 2009 that the company laid me off, and I applied for unemployment benefits for the first time. I got around $400 a week before tax in a prepaid debit card, sufficient to cover my living expenses.

By this time, the U.S. stocks behaved differently and were choppy during the day, so my original trading strategy no longer worked, and I started losing money and patience. I made more mistakes trying to figure things out and eventually lost all previous profits and more to end up closing my brokerage account at a total loss of $11,646.

Leaving Las Vegas

I shared a van ride with some other engineers located in Las Vegas to travel to the testing site in Pasadena, California. We stayed in a hotel overnight to prepare for the next day's exams. I did well on the Seismic Principles exam since my strength was in this subject, but I got bogged down in the Engineering Surveying exam and could not finish it well. Back in Las Vegas, I did not put in all the effort in my Macroeconomics class but did well enough to get a grade of A- in the end. I also noticed the instructor verbally claimed an MBA degree from Columbia University, but the university's website did not show that.

Later, I felt the need to be more educated in trading knowledge after my recent failure, so I studied through a book I previously bought, '*Technical Analysis: The Complete Resource for Financial Market Technicians.*' The book showed me a comprehensive view of the principles, history, theories, and analysis methods accumulated over the years by practitioners in this field. I found the '*fractal*' concept very interesting, which was used to describe the similar pattern of market prices over different time periods. Fractal patterns also exist in nature, in patterns of snowflakes, tree branches, and many other things.

After three years, I did not have a trophy American girlfriend and was not impressed with Las Vegas' quality of life, economy, culture, or education. There were indeed very beautiful women in the city, but they worked as lures in casinos or by themselves to attract customers for money. The city was extremely hot during the summer, severely lacked greenery, and ran short of water supply. Once, I came to eat Pho (the popular Vietnamese soup dish) at a Vietnamese restaurant, and after finding out that I was born Northern Vietnamese, a restaurant worker called me "*son of Ho Chi Minh*" and talked to me like the enemy, so I never went there again.

After searching online for different U.S. cities where I would likely be happy to settle down and could afford to live on my unemployment benefits, I decided to move to Minneapolis-Saint Paul, called the Twin Cities, in Minnesota. The unemployment rate of the Twin Cities was surprisingly under 10%, about half the unemployment rate of Las Vegas and California.

I also remembered the word '*Saint*' in the city name of Saint Petersburg in the Soviet Union, which I visited in 1987, and wondered what this mythical word meant that it was also used in America. I found a sublease available for the summer in a student-living apartment in Minneapolis and deposited the lease. I sold most of my belongings, packed only the essential items in my car, and planned a 3-day road trip from Las Vegas to Minneapolis, staying in Motel 6 along the highway at night.

Changing Career and Living in Minneapolis, Minnesota

Exploring the Twin Cities

In May 2009, I had an amazing road trip through the canyons of Utah, the mountains and hills of Colorado, the plains of Nebraska, the windmills of Iowa, and the lakes and woods of Minnesota. I came to Minneapolis, Minnesota. The sublease apartment I got was at 2508 Delaware Street Southeast, very close to the University of Minnesota (U of M) campus. I was pleased as the city looked clean, green, and peaceful and felt like a normal but cultured Midwest American city. My roommates and most apartment residents were students at the U of M, and I enjoyed living in the same community with them. I got in the mail that I passed the Seismic Principles exam but failed the Engineering Surveying exam with a raw score of 29. I chose not to take that exam again since I would have to travel to California, and now living in Minnesota, I may never need that coveted California P.E. license.

I took my time to settle down and check out the U of M campus, downtown Minneapolis, downtown Saint Paul, Como Park, and the Mall of America. After a very long time, probably since childhood, I had a great summer break, free of worry. The apartment where I lived had some community activities, and I got to know others besides my roommates. We played sand volleyball and watched the Minnesota Viking games and the Office TV series. I went to popular places in the city at night on the weekend. I also had paid off my car by this time, bought cheap personal computer parts, and learned how to build a PC for the first time. In my mind, I was still dreaming of making a lot of money to achieve financial freedom. I shared what I believed about money with one of my roommates, who was originally from Wisconsin, but unexpectedly, he responded that pursuing money was actually the root of all evil and unhappiness, which I could not comprehend how someone could have such a view.

By the end of the summer, I started looking at the job market in Minneapolis, but just like the rest of the country, companies were either laying people off or not hiring. However, I noticed one type of job that many companies always advertise and hire: the Financial Advisor job. The description of these jobs sounded very attractive to me as they did not require a related Bachelor's degree but a willingness to work hard and help people who need advice with their finances and investments. Indeed, the engineering jobs I experienced previously severely lacked social interactions or female co-workers, as the office manager at my first company, M.A. Engineering Inc., put it as "*extremely boring.*" I desired social connections with born Americans to assimilate into U.S. society and culture. I also had experience trading in the U.S. stock market and was formally educated in Economics, so it was a no-brainer that the job was a good fit for my intellectual and social interests.

Switching Career

I prepared my resume and cover letters tailored to the job of a Financial Advisor and applied to all of the entry-level jobs I found advertising online. I first got an interview with North Star Financial, located next to where I lived, but I only got a follow-up email. Then, I got into the online screening and testing from Ameriprise Financial headquarters in downtown Minneapolis. It was a tricky personality test for personal beliefs, consistency of answers, and corporate behavior. I passed this online screening and got an in-person interview where I needed to perform a proctored math test first. I did not prepare for the math test since I did not know what to be prepared for. The test required only arithmetic skills but quick eyes and hands in real-world applications of financial markets and investments. Being caught off guard, I ran out of time to understand some problems and could not finish the test after 30 minutes. I was not interviewed because I fell short of 2 correct answers to pass the test.

During this time, I registered my car with the state of Minnesota and received my owner title; however, one letter of my car model name had been misspelled. I reported this to the corresponding personnel, but ironically, she told me that was the correct spelling!

Eventually, I got in-person interviews with the Waddell & Reed Inc. office in Bloomington. The ones who interviewed me were Jason, the District Manager, and then Lori, the Managing Principal. By this time, I had already read some information online and books about a career as a Financial Advisor. I understood the nature of the job was 100% commission sales with very high turnover, and mentally prepared to do whatever it took to be successful. In the end, despite the negative of my foreign accent, Jason and Lori were convinced by my life story of success so far and my bold spirit to get clients and decided to get me on board. It was in October 2009 that I became an associate person with Waddell & Reed Inc. However, I needed to do Fingerprinting, take and pass the 3 hours 45 minutes Series 7 General Securities Representative Examination and the 2 hours 30 minutes Series 66 Uniform Combined State Law Examination to register with FINRA as a broker.

Exams and Registration

Searching online, I found an advertisement and bought study books for the Series 7 and Series 66 exams from Securities Training Corporation. I studied diligently for a month, then took and passed the Series 7 exam on November 2, scoring 80%. I studied diligently for another two weeks, then took and passed the Series 66 exam on November 19, scoring 75%. The Series 7 exam was hard due to its quantitative nature, but the Series 66 exam, even though shorter, was not any easier due to its tricky wording of the Laws.

Since a Financial Advisor could also sell certain insurances that bring in commissions, I also registered and took the Minnesota Life, Accident, and Health Insurance Exam, which required an in-person class by Kaplan, and then the Minnesota Long-Term-Care Insurance Exam, which I self-studied. These exams were easier, and I passed them without any difficulty.

After completing all paperwork and fingerprinting, I was set to sell a personal financial plan, suitable investment products according to age and risk tolerance, mostly proprietary Waddell & Reed mutual funds, and life or health or long-term-care insurance from various associated carriers. During this time, I noticed that one letter in my middle name was misspelled (not by me) in the registration with FINRA, and I reported this to the office. However, the corresponding personnel at the company's headquarters who did it refused to correct it! Jason told me it was a difficult lady in the company's compliance department that everyone had to tolerate.

Learning Sales

My first plan of attack was to target Vietnamese business owners in the Twin Cities, so I searched online and gathered their names, phone numbers, and business addresses. There were not many of them, and they were mostly restaurant businesses. I called and came presenting what I do in person, sometimes along with Jason, to those who responded initially. I did not connect with them since they were all Southern Vietnamese and generally had different personal finance and investment ideas. An established financial advisor in the office opposed me after knowing that I was prospecting one Vietnamese restaurant owner who was also her prospect.

It was during Christmas 2009 that Jason invited me to his home in West Saint Paul for dinner. The last time I had a Christmas family meal was at Don and Ruth's house in Buffalo, New York, so I accepted immediately. Jason was a nice, caring man; his wife and kids were a pleasure to be around. Even though Jason did not tell me, I felt they were a Christian family. After dinner, we played a golf video game via Nintendo Wii Sports with the kids, and to my surprise, whenever I shook the controller in my hand, it started an earthquake in the game that made it difficult to play for my opponent. This, combined with knowing my earthquake engineering education, that Jason wittily called me "*Mr. Earthquake.*"

My second marketing effort was to conduct an exhibit booth where people drop their contact information in a fishbowl for a gift card at the annual Southern Vietnamese Festival in early 2010. People were generally friendly, but one man pointed at me then talked and showed disdain. I got over a hundred contacts and called them in the evenings, presenting what I do. Some people responded positively initially but later avoided my contact after mentioning some negativity about the investment and insurance industry. I got one person, who was a white man married to a Vietnamese wife with around $250,000 in investable assets, interested enough to meet with Jason and me in the office. He could have become a good client, but I drove him away due to my lack of patience and people skills.

Picking up Girls

During this time, I contacted local guys with the same interest in practicing picking up girls via alt. seduction. fast (ASF) newsgroup over the internet, which was the original and first of its kind. After some screening and meeting in person, the guy interested in hanging out with me was Andrew, three years older than me, and he already had success with the girls.

He had invested serious time and money in live training with Real Social Dynamics, known as the world's largest dating coaching company. Andrew told me of his previous failures, his depression, and how the live training changed his life for the better. He was experimenting with coaching new guys, and I followed his lead. Andrew and I had good chemistry, and under his guidance, I put in serious efforts to approach and talk to many girls on weekend nights in popular bars and clubs in Minneapolis.

Picking up girls in nightspots was incredibly hard due to its socially competitive and chaotic environment, but I dared to try despite constant streams of failures and rejections. The most frustrating thing was the blocking from other girls or guys when the girl was responsive to my advances. Deep down, I was not truly happy with the shallow interactions, but I did not know nor had better places to meet girls. After a while, I was comfortable operating on my own and eventually succeeded in picking and following up with a girl named Katherine, who was extremely pretty in my eyes. I gave her a ride to a party organized by my apartment, and we had great chemistry and a lot of wet kisses. It was the first time in my life I fell in love with a girlfriend.

Cold Calling and Seminar

Back to my job, after running out of all Vietnamese prospects without any sales, I got an email out of nowhere selling a contact information list of around 500 local investors who were not on the National Do Not Call Registry for more than $300. They included a letter advertising experience of buyers who got clients with millions of investable assets by calling people from the list. Desperate for prospective clients and not knowing anything better, I purchased the list and called in the evenings. I found some bad phone numbers, Do Not Call numbers, and people who told me not to call back.

Some people did not reject my call and sales pitch but told me to call back later, or maybe they would invest in the future, so I kept these contacts as future prospects. After a while, I realized the contact list was likely excerpted from a national phone directory, and I used an online directory from Hennepin County Library to download a lot more random local contacts and then I called them. I worked hard calling and pitching all evenings and weekends and learned patterns of different responses from people. Sometimes, on the weekends, while I was calling through the phone numbers in the office, Jason came in with his kids as support and encouragement for my efforts. I remember one of his sons was named Noah, which sounded like a very strange old name to me.

My third marketing effort was to conduct a seminar on China's great demand to import raw materials, to attract prospective clients in a different way. The seminar invitations and presenting slides were readily prepared by Waddell & Reed. I practiced hard memorizing the slides and speaking them aloud during the day. And I called my contacts in the evenings, who were all strangers, to invite them to my seminar. After examining my seminar presentation, Lori applauded and approved me to be the speaker. However, out of all the people who said to attend, only one actually did, and despite my excellent presentation, she did not become a client after my follow-up.

Forced Resignation and Trying Again

In the end, what mattered was actual sales, not how hard one tried or how many prospects one had. By the end of April 2010, I was forced to resign despite having cold-called more than 4000 phone numbers and obtained some prospects since I did not bring in any sales, much less meeting production expectations. During an office party before I finally left the company, Jason told me, "*You don't know what you don't know,*" which struck me as very interesting and undeniably true.

Katherine and I went out to watch a Minnesota Timberwolves game after much of her playing hard to get. She was a student at Saint Catherine University and still somewhat immature, and so was I. In retrospect, the pickup scene created distrust among the people involved, and we could not communicate well. She admitted she had sex with a guy while studying in Spain in the past. She said she would become sick if she took birth control pills and wanted marriage. I let her examine my cell phone as she wanted but took it back when she got too far, and she threw a tantrum. Even though it was heartbreaking, I did not see the point of putting up with this broken communication, so I decided to move on with my life.

After six months working for Waddell & Reed, I had earned no income but gained a thick skin, some insight into financial sales, and an appetite for cold calling. I searched online, finding useful information from the registeredrep.com website, and bought an eBook about how to get hired as a broker for the four largest and globally known full-service brokerage firms called the '*wirehouses,*' which included Merrill Lynch, Morgan Stanley, Smith Barney, and UBS. The author of the eBook, a former employee at one of the wirehouses, showed insight into these firms' selection and hiring processes.

Following the guide in the book, I targeted the Merrill Lynch downtown Minneapolis office and personally emailed all the current advisors in the office asking for advice. I started compiling a phone numbers list of more than 20,000 professionals, business owners and executives, and more than 10,000 residents within the metro area and also prepared a business plan and client acquisition strategy based solely on cold calling. Then, I applied to the Merrill Lynch Practice Management Development (PMD) program and other wirehouses with a compelling cover letter of what I had done so far.

During this time, my aunt and uncle-in-law, who worked for the Vietnam Ministry of Foreign Affairs, had recently moved to downtown Ottawa, Canada, with their two children. Without the commitment of a job, I took a roundtrip flight to visit them in their apartment for a week. At first, they were still skeptical about whether I had become a U.S. permanent resident until they saw my Green card with their eyes. We drove to Montreal in Quebec province for a day, watched the 2010 FIFA world cup games on TV, and watched fireworks on Canada Day. I had a great time refreshing after the trip and was determined to push with all I got to break into the Financial Advisor career. I called and talked to Dũng, my paternal grandmother's younger brother, to get the contact information of some very wealthy Vietnamese people and include them in my business plan.

Merrill Lynch's Hiring Process

Since I already had my Series 7 and Series 66 licenses, I was waived from taking a quantitative aptitude test for the Merrill Lynch PMD program. However, I had to take a personality test in which I was asked repeatedly how many high-net-worth individuals with more than $250,000 investable assets I knew and how confident I was in successfully bringing in a lot of business quickly. Mentally prepared for this, I passed the test without any problem. The final round was an in-person interview with three different Merrill Lynch advisors in the office on the 44th floor of the Capella Tower in downtown Minneapolis.

The last interviewing advisor, also Resident Director, was James, who unexpectedly asked about my life since childhood and then tested me live with a mockup cold call. I responded very well with impromptu and absolute confidence. Then, I was asked what guidebook I use and the expected ratio of cold calls to new clients. I answered *'The Million-Dollar Financial Services Practice' by David J. Mullen Jr.*, and for every hundred talked-to contacts, I would get ten prospects, and for every ten prospects, I would get one new account.

At the end of the interview, James mentioned David Mullen was the former branch manager of this office who hired him and showed me two different salary levels, one at $50,000 and the other at $75,000, with two corresponding Production Credit hurdles that increase greatly over the course of the PMD program. Understanding the difficulty of meeting these hurdles, I chose the lesser salary. After that interview, I was asked to come to the office again to meet with the compliance officer, who asked how I chose Minneapolis and about my connections with government officials in Vietnam. A few days later, I got the job offer via email as expected, and I immediately accepted it and then withdrew from the job application process of other firms I applied to.

On the first day at work, I was called to meet with Doug, the Director and Branch Manager, for the first time. He said that out of many competitive applicants, I was hired along with a few others by narrowly winning 51% of the votes from the advisors in the office. He also commented that I was very ambitious and would be successful beyond any doubt. I did not expect such a high word for me. At the end of August 2010, I was officially registered with Merrill Lynch as a broker and investment advisor.

PMD Program

My new co-workers and I in the PMD program had weekly meetings for general instructions and training in the office by different established advisors and officers. Most of us already had work experience in financial sales from other companies, and one was the son of the most senior advisor in the office. Merrill Lynch had a cast bronze bull statue on Wall Street, and I was given a silver pin of the bull logo, which I proudly wore every day on my suits at work. There was a stark difference between the system platforms, client's wealth and portfolio analysis, market insight, analyst information, and financial products of Merrill Lynch and Waddell & Reed.

Besides all the publicly known investment products and mutual funds, there were products structured in-house using sophisticated investment vehicles and markets. There were also financial products or separately managed accounts by third-party insurance companies or money managers available only to clients at the wirehouses. The program also required everyone to study, take, and pass the Certified Financial Planner (CFP) Principles of Financial Planning exam, the first of 6 CFP exams, which I subsequently completed. The training pressed a comprehensive wealth planning and management approach, which I preached on my cold calls.

I found out in the office that people who made it through the PMD program were given assets from family members or an advisor team or inherited accounts from failed or left advisors. Even advisors who made it through the program could still make little production credits and were forced out of the firm later. I was informed that I couldn't get international clients, and I had no family members or connections in the U.S., so my odds of making it were practically none.

Yet I still believed in making it via the hard work of cold calling non-stop. It was indeed the way many established advisors made it in the past. In retrospect, I did not realize the financial services industry had been saturated with new advisors, and most qualified investors had been constantly pursued and acquired by established advisors over the years. I came to work and cold-called every day non-stop from early morning to late evening except Sunday when I had to do laundry and grocery shopping. All I got were bad numbers, not available, rejections, or already having an advisor. The best responses I got were "*call back later,*" and I accumulated these contacts as prospects.

By January 2011, Doug was suddenly let go from the company, and after a while, Mark became the new Director and Branch Manager. Mark was the former Resident Director at Merrill Lynch Wayzata office, where his brother was a top-producing financial advisor in Minnesota. He called me to his office, warning me that I would be fired if I did not meet the production credits hurdle. I was always cold-calling like a machine all the time, so there was not much else I could do about it. Everyone in the PMD program was required to show a pipeline of prospects and encouraged to team up with an established advisor in the office to help close them.

I found out that established advisors wanted somewhere from 50% to 75% of the production credits brought in, knowing full well that made it multiple times harder for the new advisor to meet hurdles, and when the new advisor failed, they kept the account. The new advisor exception was the son of the most senior advisor in the office. He did not need to prospect and was given assets to meet all the hurdles. During a small talk of compassion, a fellow advisor in the PMD program named Nathan, who had experience pastoring in the past and had some existing clients, told me, "*It's not about hard work. The rich just get richer.*"

Pushing Hard

Not being discouraged and still trying as hard as possible, I started to cold call even the Do Not Call residential numbers as advice from some established advisors was, "*Do what you need to do.*" After months of trying, I got some in-person appointments and made several avoidable mistakes. One retiree asked me to open an account during our first meeting, where I brought the marketing materials but did not bring the account paperwork since I did not expect to close that day, and the retiree backed out later. Another business owner had around $100,000 to invest, but I declined to open the account since I was taught in the recent training that an advisor could only survive to service an account of $250,000 or more. There were certain painful rejections in my cold callings because of my foreign accent. Sometimes, I was believed to be a fraud; sometimes, I was told angrily to "*go back to your country.*" Other times, lawyers tried to convict me of unlawful solicitation over the phone.

The office noticed my consistent hard work, but my results did not match the work I put in. I was reminded of my foreign accent flaw and was advised to work harder to compensate for it during the training meetings, and I acknowledged it. To save time, I ate meal-replacement protein bars all day long and drank a lot of plain water as required. Sometimes, I bought a gargantuan sandwich at the local Jimmy John's shop inside the skyway area of the Capella Tower for lunch, but I never drank soda, Coke, or Pepsi.

Yet one day, a Chartered Financial Analyst (CFA) charter holder working for one of the office's top and most senior advisors sent an email to the whole office implying someone like me stole his can of Coke in the office with a statement, "*It's not yours.*" Also, there was a backroom in the office with a couch that I usually used to nap in the early afternoon to recover my stamina for the rest of the day until late evening. After the office discovered my napping, the couch was removed, but I managed to nap on the armchair in that backroom instead.

After more months of unabated hard work, I finally opened some accounts, and independently. Via multiple phone calls, follow-ups, and appointments, I opened an account for a family with more than $750,000 in their 401(k) to partially withdraw it. Another account was opened for a financial controller to transfer over his existing account with Fidelity. I also opened a Bank of America credit card for him to consolidate the balance. These clients were far from downtown and outside the Twin Cities metro area. At this time, I was the only one in the PMD program without previous clients to open new accounts. To boost the morale of everyone in the PMD program, the office conducted an in-house recording of each person's prospecting activities on a board. After two weeks, my record showed a number of appointments and more than 3000 cold calls, which topped the board by a distance from anyone else.

More Learning

Eventually, I opened another account on my own for a business owner with a $10 million net worth in Wisconsin, more than an hour away by car from the office. He purchased a $240,000 annuity with built-in investment in selective mutual funds that guaranteed to payout 5% or more depending on investment outcome which I charged a 1% wrap fee. During this time, interest rates had been close to zero for years, and I only knew about this attractive product after talking with Greg, an established advisor in the office. Greg also disclosed to me that a top-producing female advisor in the office was churning her clients.

I wondered why he comfortably told me so and why the office did nothing about it. One night, while doing cold calling alone in the office, I got a phone call from someone representing Morgan Stanley asking if

I would like to switch companies. And there would be a bonus according to client assets and production bringing over, but I declined since I was loyal to Merrill Lynch and not an established advisor. In August 2011, the stock markets worldwide experienced a sharp drop in prices and subsequent extreme volatility.

Within Merrill Lynch, there was a discretionary investment platform for qualified financial advisors to operate in which the advisor acts as the portfolio manager to buy and sell securities without the client's consent for each trade. The titles for advisors operating on this platform in ascending order were Portfolio Advisor, Portfolio Manager, and Senior Portfolio Manager, where the Portfolio Advisor operation was limited to a set of pre-constructed portfolios. At that time, to become a Portfolio Advisor, one needed to have at least one year of experience working as a financial advisor and pass an ethics exam similar to that of the CFA Level I exam.

Interested in expanding my credentials and offering services to clients as I had been with Merrill Lynch for more than a year, I took and passed the ethics exam and applied to become a Portfolio Advisor. However, I needed approval from the compliance officer, and he denied my application, stating that I would need five years of experience. I talked with James, the office's Resident Director, about this. Subsequently, my application was approved, and I became a Portfolio Advisor.

I started reading different market and portfolio research information from Merrill Lynch analysts and came up with a long-shot market-neutral investment strategy as a response to the previous August 2011 stock markets fall and volatility. Previously, I already read about technical analysis, which studies markets' price and volume actions to make trading decisions, so I attended the meetings of the Market Technicians Association (MTA) located inside the investment banking company Piper Jaffray's downtown office within the Minneapolis

Skyway system. In these meetings, I got to know Tim, the co-chair of the Association's Minnesota chapter and a financial advisor at Royal Bank of Canada (RBC) Wealth Management.

Pride and Arrogance

In my subsequent appointment meetings with prospective clients, I used my new credentials and the market-neutral strategy as my selling point. Feeling like I had found a way to sky-high success and was filled with ambition and pride, I advertised the market risk-neutral strategy in my profile on Merrill Lynch's webpage and even changed my job title in my LinkedIn account to a hedge fund manager.

Little did I know that Merrill Lynch closely monitored their advisors' phone calls and public profiles. Mark called me to his office, informing me that I would get into trouble if I did not correct my job title on LinkedIn, and he was aware of Morgan Stanley's calling me. He talked down to me that I was just a fledgling advisor and former engineer-in-training, which was true. But with pride and arrogance, I replied that I came to get on the fast track to success. Subsequently, the office compliance officer forced me to correct my Merrill Lynch profile webpage, and I also corrected my LinkedIn profile, knowing they were my wrongdoing.

Previously, some financial advisors were terminated or switched to UBS or other banks, and the leftover clients of these advisors were distributed to advisors remaining in the office. These distributions were supposed to be fair, but I never got any account given to me, and people noticed this. This time, the top-producing female advisor in the office left to start her own company, and I was finally given a couple of accounts to call and keep the clients staying at Merrill Lynch. The only significant client from these was a senior woman, and via the phone conversation, she disclosed that previously she got letters from Merrill Lynch stating her account was churned by her advisor, which made her sleepless for three nights. I calmed her down by ensuring to put her interest first and made an in-person meeting appointment with her. However, an established advisor in the office interfered, took the lead in the appointment meeting, and made the account his.

The Downfall

To everyone's surprise, Greg and his team also left during this time and went to Morgan Stanley on the 53rd floor of the same Capella Tower. James, the office's Resident Director, moved to Pasadena, California office to become the Branch Manager there. I still kept working hard as always and started to have some appointments with high-net-worth attorneys within downtown Minneapolis, but I had not yet opened any more accounts and fell far behind the required production hurdles. Even worse, during one night of cold calling through the Do Not Call numbers, I not knowingly called an existing Merrill Lynch client of an established advisor. The client wanted to report me, and I hung up the phone. The next day, Mark called me to his office to meet him and the compliance officer. They informed me that I was terminated effective immediately and not eligible for rehire.

Nathan was very nice to give me a ride back to my apartment that day when I was fired from Merrill Lynch in November 2011. He comforted me by saying not to be sad and told me that everyone else in the PMD program would have to leave eventually except people with wealthy family connections, which was later shown to be 100% correct. At home, I was extremely devastated since I put in all I could ever do, gaining much experience and ongoing connections, to be suddenly taken away with no hope of ever getting them back. Even worse, little did I know that my hard work and unhealthy diet for long took a serious toll on my health and body.

I started getting bad acne on my skin and my face a couple of months before being terminated, and treatment prescribed by a dermatologist downtown using antibiotics did not help. Then, my lower back got seriously hurt, and I had to stay in bed for several days before I could stand up straight. Fortunately, I was eligible for unemployment and qualified for low-cost health insurance under the Affordable Care Act. I took plenty of rest, started making real meals, and exercised in the apartment gym. I also bought computer parts and built a custom liquid-cooling PC for the first time to entertain myself.

A Different Attempt

From what I learned about financial markets and portfolio management, my new inspiration and plan were to try making a career in that field, leveraging my relevant work experience as a financial advisor. However, I heard that one needs to at least clear the CFA Level I exam, which was difficult, time-consuming, and the first of 3 exams to earn the CFA Charter designation, the gold standard in asset management. I always enjoy learning new things, so I committed to studying and taking the CFA Level I and the Chartered Market Technician (CMT) Level I exam, the first of 3 exams to earn the CMT Charter designation, the gold standard in technical analysis and trading.

In April 2012, convinced by the advertisement over the internet, I went to Crutchfield Dermatology in Eagan seeking to treat my annoying acne problem. I complained that I had had this issue for 15 years without any cure, and Doctor Crutchfield promised it would be eliminated once and for all following his treatment plan. He recommended taking isotretinoin pills regularly, saying acne would worsen and I may experience depression initially then become better after a year. And I agreed, believing in him. So I diligently come to his office for regular checking and refills of my pills.

By May 2012, I passed the CMT Level I exam on the first attempt without much difficulty. Two months later, I got a passing result for my first attempt at the June 2012 CFA Level I exam. This 6-hour exam was difficult, covering ten broad topic areas of Ethical and Professional Standards, Quantitative Methods, Economics, Financial Reporting and Analysis, Corporate Finance, Portfolio Management, Equity Investments, Fixed Income, Derivatives, and Alternative Investments.

Taking a break from studying, this time, I took a roundtrip flight to visit my aunt and uncle-in-law in Ottawa, Canada, for two weeks. My back still hurt occasionally, but we managed to fly to Vancouver for a few days of the visit. We also drove to see Vancouver's breathtakingly beautiful vacation areas, watched the 2012 FIFA Euro games on TV, and watched fireworks on Canada Day. Again, I had a great time refreshing after the trip, as I did in 2010.

Back in Minneapolis, I prepared my latest finance career resume and applied to a number of entry-level analyst and trader positions I found available within the metro areas. I got a couple of responses via email, but I did not get any interviews in the end, so I committed to study and take the CMT Level II exam in October. During this time, I stayed two weeks at a house in the Stevens Squares neighborhood via Airbnb.com before moving to the new Stadium Village Flats apartment at 850 Washington Avenue Southeast. I made friends with the young owner, Eric, and one of his friends played an acoustic guitar, which inspired me to buy a cheap classical guitar at a Guitar Center store and recover some of my skills from the past. I also tried out Taekwondo and Ballroom dance clubs open to anyone at the U of M's Recreation Center.

In August 2012, I enrolled as a patient at Hennepin County Medical Center (HCMC) to fully examine my health and, subsequently, undergo a series of blood tests. These blood tests showed off the chart numbers indicating my health was in bad shape and I needed regular physical exercise and a healthy diet. By October 2012, I took and passed the CMT Level II exam on the first attempt with some difficulty. I continued applying for available entry-level finance jobs but got no results. I also contacted the Market Technicians Association, indicating my search for a job, but got no interview or referral from them. Reluctantly, I started looking for engineering jobs as the U.S. economy had generally recovered from the Great Recession of 2008.

Back to Engineering Career and Suffered Disability

Contract Job and Hobbies

Via a temporary staffing agency in downtown Minneapolis, I got a contract structural engineer job with Donaldson Company Inc. to work in their global headquarters in Bloomington. I got paid around $33 per hour without any benefits at all, and I was told the company wanted to see if it was a good fit before officially hiring someone as an employee. My job was using structural analysis and design software Risa-3D to model and design industrial steel platforms and structures for Siemens and General Electric. Three other engineers did the same line of work and gave me different assignments. I did well technically, but later, I saw some domineering attitude from management and had a conflict of personality with the supervising female engineer, so I lost interest, and they let me go as not a good fit.

During this time, after work in the evenings, besides practicing classical guitar, I also practiced Taekwondo at Grandmaster Lee's World Taekwondo Academy in Maple Grove. The monthly fee was the highest I had ever seen at $170 per month, but I still wanted to try since Grandmaster Lee had impressive qualifications and was a former assistant Olympic coach for the U.S. national team. What caught me by surprise was the undeserved high-praise introduction of me to the club by Grandmaster Lee. I noticed that certain adult members were suspicious of me, asking where I was from and what my job was. During one training day, Grandmaster Lee suddenly ordered free sparing on the spot when I was paired up with a fierce fighter who was much taller, bigger, and stronger than me. I defended myself and then counterattacked him successfully. What I found interesting was that during a conversation in the club, this fighter told me he married very young when he was 15 years old. He certainly had sex at 15, but the law did not allow marriage at that age.

After a while, I got my Yellow belt from the Taekwondo club. The facility, training, and people there were excellent, and I learned some good sparring and real-life defense techniques. There were a good number of young girls in the club, and I started to have a liking for a young female instructor, and she liked me back. I got her phone number and talked to her in the club, but Grandmaster Lee saw it and came to tap on my shoulder. I took that as a sign of disapproval, and later the girl texted me confirming that she had to keep a distance from students. I left the club after two months since the fee was too high for me and the location was far from where I lived.

Full-time Job, and Money from Family

By January 2013, I got a new full-time structural engineer job with Enclos Corp in their local office in Eagan. I got the job by applying directly online. I went through a screening process by their in-house recruiter and had to interview twice with my future manager, Bob. After some negotiation, the company only agreed to pay a $60,000 salary and a $2000 sign-in bonus. It was quite lower than my previous salary when I was working with G.C. Wallace Inc. in Las Vegas, but I accepted it as it was the only offer I got at that time. I also applied for U.S. citizenship during this time, as it was approaching five years since I got my Green Card.

I was still playing classical guitar in the evenings and started practicing Song Moo Kwan Taekwondo at the World Martial Arts Center in uptown Minneapolis. The facility and training were not as great as that of World Taekwondo Academy, but the location was close, and I only had to pay $90 per month, so I was happy.

By April 2013, I had been diligently following the treatment plan by Doctor Crutchfield for a year without fail. However, my acne did not diminish as expected, and I found myself losing hair in certain areas of my head! Once, I had to seriously hurt myself in order to remove an acne seed as hard and big as a grain of rice deep in my chest with my fingers. I complained and asked if this was due to isotretinoin pills I was taking, but Doctor Crutchfield said it was a coincidence and added to my regular visit a needle shot to my scalp to treat the hair loss. I still believed him and followed his recommendation to continue taking isotretinoin pills at a lower dosage.

At home in Vietnam, due to my parent's divorce, a valuable home that the government gave my mother for her lifetime work was sold. The arrangement was that my mother still lives in the original home in Ngoc Ha village, half the proceeds were used to purchase an apartment for my father, and the remaining half was sent to me to purchase a home in the U.S., which amounted to $200,000. I kept the money in the bank and started looking into the real estate market.

P.E. Licensure and U.S. Citizenship

At work, I was assigned to work on field fixes of anchors for curtain walls of the Jacob Javits Convention Center Renovation and then on moving mechanism and lifting of curtain walls of the National Museum of African American History and Culture. I did these well using my technical knowledge and skills with Mathcad and AutoCAD software packages. For my career progression, I needed P.E. licenses in California, Minnesota, and New York, where the company's offices and projects were located. Luckily, the only thing left in the past that I needed for my California license was to pass the Engineering Surveying exam, which after a recent change could be taken in a computer-based format at a local testing center.

So I studied, took, and passed the test this time and obtained my California P.E. license in May 2013. After some paperwork, studying 100 simple questions regarding the U.S., and a quick interview, I became a U.S. citizen on June 26, 2013. I also officially changed my legal name to Tony A Tran, which I had been using informally since my first arrival to the U.S. In August 2013, I moved back to live in the apartment building at 2508 Delaware Street Southeast.

To obtain a P.E. license in a state, one had to follow the rules and requirements of the Board of Engineering and related disciplines in that state. One thing in common was submitting documentation of engineering degree(s), verification of passing the FE and PE exams, detailed work experience history, and multiple letters of reference by other P.E. engineers. It was extremely cumbersome, awkward, and time-consuming to do this each time for each state, so the National Council of Examiners for Engineering and Surveying (NCEES) allowed an engineer with one P.E. license to establish a centralized record of all relevant information called the NCEES Record.

Once established, this Record can be updated and transmitted to all State boards. So, I proceeded with establishing my Record; however, I found out that because my bachelor's degree was earned outside of the U.S., I needed to have my degree and its entire curriculum evaluated by the NCEES Credentials Evaluation Service.

NCEES Record

Unfortunately, the Hanoi Architectural University, where I obtained my bachelor's degree, could not issue my transcript and degree in English and did not have a detailed description of its curriculum. For the next several months, I spent available time looking up original Vietnamese textbooks and course contents to write a detailed description of each course, degree, and transcript in bilingual Vietnamese and English. Then, these documents were submitted to Hanoi Architectural University for verification and sent directly to NCEES Credentials Evaluation Service. After the evaluation, my 5-year bachelor's degree program met the NCEES Engineering Education Standard.

However, when looking into education credits given to foreign degrees by Minnesota and New York Boards, my Bachelor's degree, despite meeting NCEES standards, only counted as two years, and with 1-year education credit given to my U.S. Master's degree, my education credits were still one year short compared with someone with an ABET-accredited 4-year U.S. Bachelor degree.

From the feedback of several engineers in the company, for a New York license, despite NCEES Record, one would still have to use their paper-based forms separately to handwrite details of work experience, then mail to reference P.E. engineers for verification and mailing directly to the New York Board. The general consensus of engineers in the company was that there should be only one P.E. license that could be used nationally rather than the bureaucratic process of applying, maintaining, and paying the renewal fee for many licenses in many states.

During this time, I also talked with Mat, a recently hired drafter who was personable, regarding the continued oil leakage disaster from British Petroleum (BP) in the Gulf of Mexico. During the conversation, Mat stoically told me, "*The world is corrupt,*" which struck me as something I could subtly feel but was too busy with life and worries to discern. And why is the world corrupt?

Expectations of the Job

I was assigned to help with the 625 West 57th Street New York City project during these times at work. This building had a unique, geometrically complex, and odd curtain walls design for an architectural reason. So, each connection, anchor, embed, and related component, which were many, had different and odd orientations and loadings. After manually doing the structural design and coordinating its components geometrically together a few times using Mathcad, I figured it would be more accurate and robustly solved to normalize and put these in matrix forms where everything was systematically coordinated, much easier to modify the original design inputs and immediately see structural checking results. I implemented this solution successfully and was positively recognized by Bob and the company.

I noticed that engineers and drafters were regularly asked to work extra hours on Saturdays to catch up with the projects' schedule, which always seemed behind. Fortunately, I only had a California P.E. license and could not take on the lead engineer role for East Coast projects, and I could skip working extras for the time being. The lead engineers that I knew worked long hours. Some seemed to be active from 4 AM up to midnight. Apparently, the company's management wanted its employees to only have work-related goals. However, Bob said he would like people to have personal goals outside of work also and showed his support for my Taekwondo practice.

There was only one female engineer around my work area that I usually chatted with, but she was engaged and got married shortly after. Knowing that I was single without any real social connections in the

U.S., to my surprise, Bob expressed support for my desire to have an American girlfriend or future wife. But where could I find her?

Difficulties in Life and Work

I still put in serious efforts and went out by myself as regularly as I could on weekend nights to popular places in Minneapolis. What I learned from the acknowledged masters of picking up girls has always been proven correct: girls are attracted to the talkative, good-looking alpha male who is the center of attention. It was very difficult to do in practice, and only once in a while, with my best looks and confidence, I pulled it off.

However, I could never overcome the subsequent blocking of other people that happened every time. People said I did not know the girl, got in between the girl and me, or belittled me as an Asian or foreign guy. Once, a girl was physically pulled away from me by other people when we started walking home hand in hand. Another time, the girl's girlfriend, in her jealousy, threw away her driver's license so that she could not follow up with me after we had kissed and exchanged phone numbers last time.

Professional engineering work, in its essence, has no social interactions but rigorous thinking and analysis in the engineer's brain like a computer chip doing calculations non-stop for hours and getting hot. Being silly and not taking work etiquette seriously, I mistakenly picked on some other engineers for fun at work. It resulted in me being disciplined by Bob, and I made a serious effort to correct myself. I was still doing fine technically, so later, I was assigned to work on the New York South Street Seaport Pier 17 Renovation project with more responsibilities closer to that of a lead engineer. Based on preliminary sale models in the finite element analysis software Strand7, I worked on structural modeling and design of the project's mock-up and final curtain Wall-type A and Wall-type B.

After work in the evenings, I practiced Taekwondo at the World Martial Arts Center twice a week and leveled up my belt ranks. I focused on practicing classical guitar the remaining weekday evenings, recovered all my lost skills, and advanced some more. I ordered a semi-professional classical guitar imported from Spain for $4,000 and loved playing it. I failed to realize, like during my time working for Merrill Lynch, I was pushing my body hard with work and all these activities without adequate rest, and the inevitable happened again.

Serious Back Injury

On the last weekend of January 2014, while I was lifting a laundry basket inside my apartment, I fell down on the floor with pain in my lower back and numbness in my left leg, and I could not straighten out my lower back. The next Monday, I reported the incident to my company, and with the help of my two roommates, I came to HCMC Hospital for an examination. I also stopped going to Doctor Crutchfield for my acne treatment since it had been almost two years, but it still did not work.

I underwent X-ray, computed tomography (CT), and magnetic resonance imaging (MRI) scans at the hospital for the next few weeks. I used my two weeks of sick leave and then unpaid leave from work to stay home and rest in bed most of the time. I used a large plastic chopping board under my back while lying on the bed, and it helped relieve the pain and straightened my lower back. Results from the scans showed a compression deformity, wedge deformity with chronic appearing, degenerative disc, large broad-based bulge, and pinched nerves, among other things.

My primary care doctor verified my short-term disability and later sent medical documents and recommendations to my company. Shortly after, the company sent me a letter outlining the required physical fitness for employees, stating I would be terminated if not able to resume working quickly. By that time, I had reasonably recovered but not fully, so I returned to work before the deadline by the company. The company provided me with a new chair with a specific back support area, and I got a little more than $1000 from disability insurance after some elimination period.

Unusual Connections

During a month of my absence from work, the progress on the New York South Street Seaport Pier 17 Renovation project was maintained by other engineers. I tried my best to catch up with the project, but I got tired much sooner than I did before the back injury incident. There were also some personnel changes and re-arrangement of working groups in the office. I noticed that when the senior drafter and curtain wall designer, who was recently assigned to my group area, asked Bob some technical questions, Bob always answered, "*It's in the Bible. It's in the Bible.*"

I understood that in the steel construction industry, the Steel Construction Manual that everyone uses, a very thick leather-bound book, was considered the *Bible* to have correct answers for all related things. But from Bob's manner of stressing it, I felt like he also suggested answers from the actual Bible for other life questions.

For the next few months, I kept hanging on to my job even though I usually felt tired soon, and sometimes I went home early to rest. I started to underperform, made some uncharacteristic mistakes, and felt sad that my acne problem only worsened. What I never expected and almost forgot about occurred during this time. Out of nowhere, I got an email from Thur, my first crush in Vietnam, who mockingly told my face bye-bye ten years ago and subsequently married her boyfriend.

She indicated in her email that via a Vietnamese acquaintance of mine, she knew that I had recently become a U.S. permanent resident (previously, I let that acquaintance know that I had become a U.S. citizen) and asked if I had a wife with kids. She expected that I would travel to Vietnam and talk with her about long-term things and put a smiley at the end of the email. In my anger and disgust, I deleted the email and blocked its address. It was clear that she only wanted my new status, disregarding genuine love and marital status, and did not believe in me.

Fired and Other Life Lessons

In June 2014, what I had been anticipating finally happened. I was called into a meeting with an executive and was informed that I was fired for a business reason due to my performance. A few weeks after being let go, I received in the mail documents from the company offering me $3000 to sign a letter that I would not seek any legal action against the company. I signed the document and subsequently received the money.

In July 2014, 1st St. NW Technical Staffing contacted me, who found my resume online and offered me an interview for a contract job, potentially leading to permanent hire. Not having any other choices, I agreed on a pay rate of $34 per hour without any benefits, then interviewed and accepted the job to work for Greg, the owner of Structural Design Associates Inc. in Champlin.

Using my skills with Risa-3D, I performed structural modeling and analysis of various new and existing building systems, including some car dealership buildings. Then, I designed the buildings' gravity and lateral resisting systems, including steel frames and braces, masonry and wood shear walls, connections, base plates, piers, and foundations. I also prepared project reports and structural sketches for the drafter.

After a month, I helped Greg catch up with where he needed to be, and then I was told to look for new work elsewhere. I reported this to 1st St. NW Technical Staffing, and they started looking for other assignments for me. I also filed an unemployment claim with the state. Subsequently, my application was approved, and the Determination of Eligibility letter stated, "*Therefore, employment with a staffing service is not suitable employment for the applicant per MN statute...The applicant was discharged for reasons other than employment misconduct upon completing the job assignment with the staffing service.*"

During this time, I kept looking around the local housing market but experienced hard selling pressures from some real estate agents. They just wanted me to sign their buyer-broker agreement without any specifics. One actually sent me a blank agreement to sign, and when I refused, he got mad at me over the phone. After a while, I decided to hold on to buying a home since I felt I would be lonely in a house with a lot of maintenance work.

Newfound Interest and Business

In August 2014, after building a new liquid cooling computer and testing its performance, I found a crowdfunded video game called Star Citizen being developed by Cloud Imperium Games, founded by Chris Roberts, a veteran and visionary space simulator game designer.

I was very impressed by the game's potential, so I purchased a game package pledge, which allowed access to Alpha testing of the game with the promise of a future spaceship I selected from available design concepts and the full game release in the future. I also chose for myself an online avatar portraying the head of a white lion that I think is my spirit animal.

Looking for work, I found an independent structural engineer role advertisement on the local Craigslist website. I responded to the advertisement and later met with John, founder of Veteran Construction Services PLLC. We agreed to work together starting September 2014, and I registered with the state of Minnesota my business TATran Corp, for that purpose. My company's role was a sub-consultant providing structural designs and reports via email for John's company. John was responsible for sales, bringing in business, reviewing, and providing engineering stamps as a licensed P.E. in Minnesota.

The work involved various steel and aluminum commercial structures in the metro area, including stairs, ladders, mezzanines, gates, barriers, and framing connections. After each structural report, I was paid a lump sum as John said, after he had taken a 25% management overhead. I bought a Risa-3D standalone license for $3000 and built proprietary Excel spreadsheets for structural modeling, calculation, and report presentations. I enjoyed not having a commute, a flexible schedule, and owning all the tools and equipment necessary for my business. I also resumed practicing classical guitar.

Visiting Home in Vietnam

I no longer had any restrictions in traveling and living inside or outside of the U.S., and with the ability to work remotely, I decided to visit family members and friends in Vietnam for the first time after ten years. After a day-long flight, I arrived in Hanoi near the end of November 2014. The city had developed and expanded greatly, and I still recognized old streets and buildings, but they just looked tiny and unorganized.

My father had a car and, with other family members, took me from the airport to stay at my aunt and uncle-in-law's house at 5 Phan Boi Chau Street. I brought some iPhones, multivitamins, nutritional supplements, and $100 bills as gifts for people. Everyone was well, and my grandmother was still in good health since the cure of her illness more than ten years before, except she had developed Alzheimer's symptoms recently.

First, I met my faithful friends Hải and Thủy, both married with small kids and were successful in their careers. Thủy was a heart surgeon with specialized training in France, and Hải was running his own architectural firm and still kept the classical guitar I gave him before coming to the U.S. While giving me a ride on his motorcycle through Nha Tho Street in Hanoi, Thủy showed me the old Big Cathedral building built by the French colonial government was being enclosed by metal barriers, and he commented how badly religion was treated.

Later, I met most of my family members and friends from childhood. Trung returned to Hanoi from Germany years ago and was married with a small kid. The only close friend I tried to see but couldn't was Sơn, and I heard he got into financial problems from the Vietnamese stock market. My mother and father each prepared a feast for me independently. My mother's feast was at our original home in Ngoc Ha village with her family members. My father and mother-in-law's feast was with coworkers from Hanoi University of Mining and Geology, where I met with the University's retired Communist Party Secretary.

After showing the retired Secretary my U.S. Passport and my own business card, he acknowledged my self-dependence and advised me to marry a white and not a black American woman. Clearly, the U.S. value system truly influenced Vietnamese people's perceived values. Before flying back to the U.S. near the end of December 2014, I talked with my father regarding how to use the money he sent me to buy a home, and my father said the ownership was mine with full control to use it how I see fit.

Dabbling in the Option Market

Back in Minneapolis, I was still providing engineering services to John as usual, and at that time, he had another independent structural engineer working for him. By January 2015, I deposited the $200,000 to my brokerage account with Interactive Broker instead of buying a home. I performed the market-neutral strategy I devised since my days with Merrill Lynch using equity research from Value Line, Inc., which could be accessed for free from Hennepin County Library.

For a month, the strategy worked fine, but then I found and read an article about options and their very high return potentials. I decided to try out a small option position, and quickly, it profited much more than my current strategy. Fascinated by this discovery, in March 2015, I found a pair of NLNK put and call options far out-of-the-money yet highly priced and could be hedged against each other. I went all in selling these two options naked and, by their expiration date in April, profited over $115,000. These extremely profitable trades convinced me I would become rich quickly, and I continued with this new strategy.

Lost All the Money and Tried Again in Life

Success and Overconfidence

For the next several months, I kept trading options very well with more sudden volatility of the underlying equities but I successfully cut losses or exited positions in time. I felt like I was worth what I was making, and the only thing I lacked was success with women. So, I used the so-called '*escort service*' from eros.com a couple of times. I was foolish enough to go through all the required verification of my identity and business to use that service.

I stopped working with John of Veteran Construction Services PLLC. I also resumed practicing Taekwondo at the World Martial Arts Center. However, I quickly realized that I had lost a lot of flexibility in my hip joints, and my right leg could not open well to the side.

By July 2015, I had more than doubled my money to around $460,000 and then withdrew the original $200,000 capital from the brokerage account to reduce position size. At that time, I also became overconfident in my ability and felt invulnerable in what I was doing. After exiting some not-profitable trade positions, I saw an apparently lucrative opportunity in ANAC where its far out-of-the-money, yet highly-priced options were about to expire, and I went all in and even more aggressively than ever, selling these naked.

Early the next Monday, I suddenly got a call from Interactive Broker informing me that my brokerage account imploded in a deep negative balance and I needed to make a deposit to cover it fully, or other legal actions would follow. What I found was that a drug by ANAC in clinical trials had just gotten positive phase 3 results, and its stock price had more than doubled overnight. Emotionally devastated, I cut losses and exited my positions with a loss of more than $300,000. Fortunately, I still had the original $200,000 in the bank and deposited it back into my brokerage account. After covering around $40,000 negative balance, the account came in at around $160,000.

I had been talking with my father and my aunt in Vietnam over the Internet about my trading results since the beginning of my winning trades, and they were also informed of this loss. By this time, I realized my lack of complete knowledge about the risks of the underlying equities and fearfully spent time reconsidering my trading strategy and position sizes.

Unusual Connections

By the end of August 2015, I moved to live in the newly constructed apartment building WaHu with new roommates at 1016 Washington Avenue Southeast. I also resumed trading options with much smaller position sizes and screened out catalysts that could cause sudden price movement. The apartment building had a very nice and large community area with tables and kitchen countertops, and I found a poster inviting residents to come next Friday for free food and fun games.

I came to the party as advertised and was unbelievably surprised that hot and delicious Vietnamese dishes were served! These were followed by incredibly fun and interactive in-person games I had never played before. Even more pleasant were the genuine and caring hearts of the women conducting the party, JaNae and Heather. I could not believe in what I saw when Heather, a white young American woman, somehow brought with her all the bowls and chopsticks and made the dishes just like my grandmother did! She cleaned the party up at the end, gathered everything, and drove back late in the evening to her place in Saint Paul.

Since that first party, I was hooked and always attended the event, which was called English Club, every two weeks on Friday evenings from 6 PM to 9 PM. There were a few more held at my apartment building, then later, all of the events were held in the basement of Stadium Village Church a few blocks away.

At English Club, I met a lot of new people, both international students from different countries as well as American students attending the U of M. There were different foods served each time with different games and discussions for people to get to know each other and it was a blast for me every time.

Other Developments

My trading was also doing well, with much smaller but steady profits. In September 2015, inspired by my hard-fought solo victory over 18 waves of Vanduul Swarm in the game Star Citizen, I started an organization within the game called Vanduul Conquerors. The Vanduul is a powerful evil alien race oppressing the human race in the Star Citizen universe, and I wanted to conquer them.

By October 2015, I had recovered my original capital of $200,000 and moved all the money into a brokerage account under my business name. I also started attending World Taekwondo Academy in Saint Paul to further my martial arts training. The facility was nice and large with a reasonable $120 monthly fee, and Master Amacher, the location's business owner, was an excellent coach.

By December 2015, using my initial P.E. license in California and my up-to-date NCEES record, I applied and obtained my Minnesota P.E. license by comity. I also finished the year 2015 with more than $42,000 in trading profits under my business name. It was an excellent, more than 20% return on original capital but at the expense of extreme volatility, which I considered a necessary learning experience.

During this time, I noticed an interesting thing about one of my roommates, who was a white American young man. He was a graduate student in the combined Master of Business Administration (MBA) and Juris Doctor (JD) program at the U of M. I thought of him as a street-smart guy with a lot of potential for success in a business or political career. One day, I saw him bring a young girl into his room, and I could overhear them. I heard loud music turned on in his room, but at the same time, I still could hear the girl's moaning during sex.

Again and again, my trading success quickly became my detrimental weakness as I thought I had mastered my trading craft over the years.

Lost Almost All

In January 2016, there was an anticipation of an interest rate increase set by the U.S. Federal Reserve that caused unusual volatility in the financial markets. Thinking that my trading activity might be affected, my father asked me how I was doing over the phone, and I assured him I could still make steady profits regardless of the situation.

At that time, I was shorting a naked out-of-the-money put option in NHTC that would expire soon. But strangely, for no apparent reason, the NHTC stock price kept going down, not suddenly but like down a deep valley.

Normally, in a situation like this, I cut my losses and exited the position timely, but this time, I decided to fight the price trend as I was determined not to lose! I doubled down in my existing positions and wired in additional $15,000 capital, hoping the options would expire before the downtrend price caught up with it.

Contrary to what I hoped, the next day, NHTC stock price kept going down even more, and prices of the naked put option I was shorting had more than doubled. Since I initially opened the brokerage account with more than $100,000 in liquid assets, it was qualified for trading on a large margin called portfolio margin. However, this margin requirement varied and was extremely sensitive to certain situations like I was in, and the account started automatically buying back my naked option positions to meet the margin requirement. By buying back at the worst price possible, the account incurred a significant realized loss and reduced margin, which then required more buying back.

I was just sitting and watching like a deer in the headlights the whole domino effect and forced liquidation of my account that day. By the end of the trading day, my total net loss was more than $178,000 since inception, and I became far from having enough capital to trade on margin for my trading strategy.

It was the first time in my life I cried long and hard for the loss of a lifetime opportunity, and the fault was squarely on me. When I slept at night, I sweated and wet my whole pillow. I informed my father and family members of the loss, and instead of blaming me, my father encouraged me to make a fresh start in life.

Pursuing What Already Lost

Subsequently, I saw an online advertisement from The Rosen Law Firm P.A. about a class action lawsuit against Natural Health Trends Corp (NHTC). From what I read, NHTC had an operation in China that was deemed illegal by the Chinese authority, but investors were not informed of this information, resulting in an unexpected loss of value in NHTC stocks.

After contacting The Rosen Law Firm, I agreed to participate in the lawsuit with them as a Plaintiff and provided them with the necessary information. Reading information online about this type of lawsuit, I understood that it takes years, and after legal fees, only a fraction of the loss would be recovered for investors if they won the case.

I also stopped going to the World Martial Arts Center after earning my Brown belt there and concentrated my training at the World Taekwondo Academy in Saint Paul only.

After a month of sorrow and regret from the loss, I decided to register, then study and take the June 2016 CFA Level II exam. The standard registration fee was $860; no refund would be given even if the examinee did not take the exam. I paid the fee and registered in 2015 but did not study or take the exam.

Passing the CFA Level II exam was generally considered the most difficult hurdle to earning the CFA Charter designation and proof of solid knowledge for an entry-level financial or security analyst job. The study material for Level II was almost double in depth and difficulty compared to that of Level I, with a heavy emphasis on Equity Investments and Financial Reporting and Analysis.

The last time I studied financial material was in 2012, and I only had more than three months before the coming exam date, so I put aside most of my time for studying except for practicing Taekwondo and attending English Club regularly. I did not work through the curriculum materials provided by the CFA Institute, which was very long, but I used Wiley's study guide to save time.

After the exam, I felt like I had performed decently and had a chance of passing, but when I received the result near the end of July, I failed with a score band 10. I underperformed in the heaviest-weighted topics of Equity Investments and Financial Reporting and Analysis and I was in the top 10% of the examinees who did not pass. I realized that I learned a lot but still needed a more thorough study to pass this difficult exam.

Business and Life Adjustments

Looking forward, I decided to use my marketing skill and experience as a financial advisor in the past to focus on finding direct customers for my engineering consulting business. I advertised locally on craigslist.org and searched and contacted local companies that would need my engineering services.

After a while, I got some leads and inquiries, and they were from random homeowners, small contractors, and metal fabricators. I charged $120 per hour and started doing home structural inspections and reports.

Being aware of my bad health in 2012, I constantly found ways to improve my diet and practice Taekwondo as regular exercise. I found that even though more expensive, organic foods were clearly better in quality, taste, and healthy. I avoided fast foods, red meat, processed food, sugar, and salt. Eventually, my regular diet included steamed wild-caught salmon and organic veggies or squashes, and I drank only filtered water. Previously, I baked farmed salmon using the oven, which always oozed a lot of fat, and the meat was pale and tasteless. I also took the multivitamin supplement and ate at least one organic apple and many ripe pitted olives daily.

Not having a commute with flexible time working at home and regular Taekwondo training, I could feel much improvement in my health and body. At the end of September 2016, my blood test result from HCMC showed a drastic improvement compared to the year 2012's test result. For instance, my Cholesterol level went from 238 (normal range 0-200 mg/dL) to 152, and my Triglyceride level went from 312 (normal range <=150 mg/dL) to 44.

At the English Club, many people came and went each time, but after a while, I noticed two regular American young men, Adam and Josh S., who were genuinely caring and pleasant to interact with. After the last English Club event of the year in December 2016, Adam and Josh S. invited me to a traditional American Christmas party at a place I had never been to, which was Sojourn Campus Church.

There, I met a large group of white American people, including families of parents with small children and many U of M students. I was uniquely impressed with the family-like atmosphere and the way students gathered in a circle, singing religious songs filled with peace and joy.

Despite feeling this was what I wanted for my life, I wondered how the students could have genuine religious beliefs, which I considered ancient myths, and studied science, which taught contrary to that.

This young mechanical engineering student, who I later came to know as Paul E., explained with a warm heart that religious beliefs and science do not have to be exclusive. It was the first time I heard about this proposition, and I believed Paul was sincere, but that was far from convincing me.

I registered early for the June 2017 CFA Level II exam, and this time, I studied and worked through the curriculum materials provided by the CFA Institute. In my engineering consulting business, besides doing home inspections, I also did residential remodeling and structural design for some local metal fabricators. However, the business was slow, and there were certain small contractors and homeowners who did not pay for my work, so I made little money.

Organization in Star Citizen

On weekends, I diligently played Star Citizen's newly released alpha version of its universe and worked hard on recruiting and training members for my Vanduul Conquerors organization in the game, just like when I worked hard as a financial advisor prospecting for clients.

I spent several thousand USD buying multi-crew military ships, including a Javelin-Class Destroyer, the most coveted and powerful ship a player could purchase. The Javelin and most ships were only in the concept stage, but I used a fly-ready multi-crew military ship to recruit and train members very effectively via Discord, a popular Voice over Internet Protocol software, and my organization grew steadily in numbers.

By April 2017, my gaming organization had grown to more than two hundred members and attracted good players for its regular multi-crew play and vision for a glorious future. However, at that time, I did not have experience in managing players who were random young adult gamers based in the U.S., Canada, and Europe.

There was this player based in Norway that I recently recruited, but he was jealous of my success and considered me a foreigner because of my accent, and he secretly plotted and persuaded some other useless players to rebel against me using false accusations.

After I had expelled these bad members, things kept going well for a while, but later, even my good players started wandering away from multi-crew play, which was the organization's identity. The multi-crew play was the most difficult thing to do in the game since it required discipline and precise coordination akin to that in the military. Not seeing the point of giving up on the multi-crew play, I insisted on it, and then all my active members left my organization to join another rising organization with the promise of doing everything a member pleases except violating the laws.

I was devastated about the loss but determined to rebuild the organization with non-compromising values and rules to focus on multi-crew play using capital ships to conquer the powerful and evil alien Vanduul in the future.

After a while, the leader of the other rising organization informed me that one of my previous members impersonated me, using my avatar, to ignite a war between the two organizations.

Moreover, a newly recruited member of my organization reported to me that two outside players contacted him, saying bad things about my organization and persuading him to leave. He even showed me their avatar pictures, and I recognized two previous rebellious members I had expelled.

However, strikingly in their new avatar pictures were their glaring red eyes full of evil spirits, so I had to delete them from my sight. Subsequently, I asked all my newly recruited members to hide their player profiles on the organization's website and made our Discord server private to prevent outside influence. I also created another Star Citizen account for security and backup reasons under the name TidusSr.

Another Try to Switch Career

Near the end of July 2017, I got the result that I passed the CFA Level II exam with flying colors. I scored >70% in the majority of topics, including Equity Investments and Financial Reporting and Analysis.

Optimistic with this new qualification, I updated my resume and applied to many relevant financial jobs I found online, many of which were from local banks, including Wells Fargo, Ameriprise Financial, RBC, and U.S. Bancorp.

I applied diligently to hundreds of entry-level openings that I was clearly qualified for but only got one interview with Ameriprise Financial. Eventually, I was not hired just to find out later the position was still not filled and was advertised again.

I reached out to people I knew from the MTA, and after being referred, I got one phone interview with a Wells Fargo hiring manager for a position requiring two years of experience that fitted my qualifications very well, according to the description.

The hiring manager even commented that he really liked my qualifications and progress in the CFA program, just to deny my application for lack of experience later. I subsequently found and applied to the same job that did not require any prior experience, but I never got any interview.

I reached out to Tim, the RBC financial advisor and former co-chair of the MTA's Minnesota Chapter, whom I knew while working for Merrill Lynch. Tim invited me to his office in downtown Saint Paul and wholeheartedly wanted to help me. He introduced me to a regional investment wholesaler and called the RBC hiring manager as my reference for a position I was interviewing for.

According to the wholesaler, he did not know of any relevant opening within his influence in the Twin Cities but knew of positions paying a $120,000 salary but requiring a 100-hour workweek and full CFA designation, which I did not have. He also was not impressed with engineers' social life, saying, "*Engineers only play with AutoCAD.*"

I got through several rounds of interviews for the position at RBC, but eventually, the hiring manager informed me that they decided to hire someone internally instead.

After trying some more without getting any job offer, I realized it was not because of my qualifications, ability, experience, or willingness to work but because I did not fit into the hiring molds that these companies would only accept.

Right or Wrong?

In August 2017, I obtained my Red belt at the World Taekwondo Academy in Saint Paul. Even though my physicality and skills were good, my body fell short of good flexibility, especially my right leg, which could not open well to the side. So, I decided not to pursue a higher belt but focus hard on remedying these physical limitations first.

I had been with the club for two years and naturally developed mutual affection with a couple of female members, including a previous instructor, but Master Amacher had to tease me by saying, "*White girl, white girl.*" I liked Master Amacher no less than anyone in the club, and he was good-hearted, but it made me wonder what's wrong with this type of thinking.

Only after coming to the U.S. that I learned about the existence of lesbians and gays, and if people make it hard for a guy or girl to find an opposite sex of their preference, isn't it pushing them toward unorthodox sexual orientation, if any? A few months later, after Master Amacher got married, many members including myself left the club, and the club closed.

At English Club, I also got to know Frank, a senior citizen and officer with Cru, which I later knew as a Christian organization. Frank was nice and invited everyone to his home and Cru building in Dinkytown several times for fellowship, free food, and a Christian history and holiday presentation. But from a conversation, I let Frank know I was doing my own engineering consulting and was much older than a student. Then Frank changed his attitude toward me, and I could tell he disliked having me around.

One evening after an English Club meeting, Frank aggressively asked me, "*Are you a Christian, Tony?*" I could tell he was looking for a reason to eject me. I was cool and honestly answered, "*No, I am not.*" And before things got heated, Adam peacefully interfered, saying that everyone was welcome at the English Club. Nevertheless, Frank said boldly, "*Evolution is not true. A tree over there never evolves into a human.*" So I explained to Frank that I believed in evolution as a truth widely accepted and taught in schools worldwide, but it also struck me that Frank got a point, and he was very certain in his belief.

Another time at English Club, during a free conversation, I talked about how the existence of the universe we live in can be explained by an infinite number of parallel but different universes of all possibilities. However, a random young American female attendee sharply rebuked me that there was no proof for that. I did not expect this response from her at all, and it struck me that she was correct. True science needs verification via observation and experiment, and there is no way we can do this with other universes we do not live in.

Involved with Christian Friends

By this time, I had made more American friends within the English Club who were members and staff of the U of M Cru, U of M Navigators, and Bethlehem Baptist Church's Campus Outreach, which I later knew as all Christian organizations.

Sometimes, after English Club, we played Frisbee brought by Christine, Noah, and other regular members. Christine also invited me to play

Frisbee with the U of M Navigators weekly and attend some of their parties, and I got to know other U of M Navigators members and staff who did not go to the English Club. Among these Navigators members, I noticed Kristin, a tall blonde, pleasant in personality and beautiful in my eyes, similar to Brittany I met many years ago in Buffalo, New York.

In October 2017, via my connection with Cru and Navigators, I learned about their annual fall retreats for a weekend at the Association Retreat Center (ARC) located in Osceola, Wisconsin. I had never had any retreat like that my whole life, and out of curiosity and desire to socialize, I registered for both. I was given a ride in a group to the Cru retreat, and there, I met a large people group, including Cru staff and students from different universities in the Midwest.

In my first group discussion, Dakota was a U of M student leader and a regular at the English Club, a female student whom I later knew as Katelyn, and a few others. They discussed how their lives were directed and corresponded to God, which baffled me, and it was clear I had no clue.

Later, a female speaker gave a talk in front of all the retreat attendants about a person's identity being solely determined by God and not by any social standards. I had never heard anything like that, and it resonated with me deeply as I recalled all the ups and downs in my life to pursue an identity of success thus far.

The activities at the retreat were simple but well organized, including group meals and shared snacks, large group religious talks and singing, small groups learning of different religious topics, sports activities, game nights, and a dance party.

There were a couple of different activities for international students and me in a group called Bridges International that was not religious. What impressed me most was the genuine connection and friendship from many strangers I had never experienced before. There, I met Gabriel and Trevor, full of unusual peace and joy, and they treated me like their brother. However, not everyone was like that.

In the bunk bed room where I slept along with other international students at night, there was a young American man who said he was born and raised in a church and always listened to worship songs. But when I returned to the room one night to sleep, the door was locked, and I could not get in. Luckily, Gabriel and Trevor noticed me outside and helped to remove the window air conditioner so that I could climb in via the opening, and they commented what kind of roommate did this. Inside the room, all the international students were gone, and only the young religious American man was sleeping in his bed.

Became Agnostic

Once, during lunchtime, I joined the long table with a group of gregarious strangers whom I later knew their names, including Josh L. and Jenna. After some conversations, Jenna asked me, "*Who do you think Jesus is?*" After some guessing, I answered, "*I think he is a prophet.*" Then Josh said, "*So people had to make animal sacrifices in the past, but because of Jesus, we no longer have to do that.*" I did not understand why Josh explained these things and what animal sacrifices have anything to do with God.

On the morning of the retreat's last day, Heather and a Cru senior staff directed me and some international students to a separate area where they presented various playing cards showing different types of beliefs for comparison. These were indeed quite eye-opening as they showed the nature of my current belief: that everything conforms to the universe's natural laws. However, I could not argue against the possibility of the Christian belief that God, the creator of the universe, is transcendent outside of space, time, and matter.

Seeing the change in my mind, Heather asked, "*So you believe now?*" And I admitted I had become agnostic about the existence of God at that moment. Then Heather added a comment that kept me pondering for a long time, "*All the crimes and wrongdoings will be punished justly by God in the end.*"

The week after the Cru retreat, I found on Facebook an event called One Church on Saturday night, organized by the U of M students at Stadium Village Church, where I went for English Club, so I decided to go. There, I met many of the same people at the Cru retreat, including Katelyn and Josh L., who performed worship singing.

Grace with the Navigators and a regular at the English Club also attended that day. After the worship, I asked Grace how she knew these things about God were true, and she said, "*Because it's in the Bible,*" which I found not convincing at all as a form of circular reasoning.

I liked Josh's singing a lot, but I also expressed that I did not see the logic in what was worshiped here, and Josh disappointingly said, "*So you need logic!*"

I then asked Katelyn how she could believe, and she answered, "*You just choose to believe,*" but she also said because the Bible correctly told the true nature of humans and asked me if there is anyone who never does anything morally wrong like telling a lie. This struck me as a deep, indisputable hidden truth.

Believing in Jesus Christ and Digging for Truth

Questioning Christian Belief

During the next English Club event, I started to have many questions about Christianity for my American friends. And Daniel, a regular at the club who I later knew as a student at Bethlehem College and Seminary, asked to pray for me. It was the first time someone prayed for me, and I sincerely submitted to his prayer, seeking understanding.

A couple of days just before the Navigators fall retreat, called The Weekender, I got a call from Adam telling me he was a leader with the Navigators and basically, I was not supposed to be there and would get a refund of the registration fee. Hearing what Adam told me, I became angry because I had already talked with several Navigators friends that I was going to, and why the exclusivity?

So I insisted I must go, and Adam yielded to my demand, saying he now feels comfortable about me going. Giving me a ride to the retreat was Ted, a good-hearted regular at English Club whom I knew well and played Frisbee with. Another Navigators member sharing the ride with us was Jonathan, who I did not know and had a long beard unlike anyone else. I also noticed Jonathan had always been around Kristin wherever she went. During the ride, I asked Ted questions about Christianity and his view on evolution. Ted explained most Christians are nominal, and only microevolution was observed, but macroevolution has never been observed. It was the first time I heard about these things, and even though I believed in macroevolution, I knew Ted was intelligent and educated in science as a chemical engineering student at the U of M.

The activities at The Weekender were very similar to that of the Cru Fall Retreat, but there was no separate track for non-believers. I was quite comfortable going along since I had been here just two weeks before and already knew many people from the English Club and the Navigators. I participated in the Frisbee tournament with the U of M team, whom I played with previously. It was a blast, and we won third place.

During lunchtime, a staff member I did not know came and sat down next to me and asked, "*What's your religious background?*" I could tell he was screening me out, and I answered that my whole family had no religious beliefs. Then he asked, "*What was taught in the teaching today?*" Indeed, many things I heard here were for the first time, and the talk by the large-group speaker also resonated with me deeply. So, I answered it was about God's love for people, that I received genuine love from my friends here, and this love indeed comes from God. Ben and his wife Emily, my Frisbee teammates at the tournament, overheard the conversation, testified that I played with them, so the staff member no longer screened me out.

During The Weekender, questions just kept popping up in my mind, and I talked to different friends for answers. It seemed I got a bit of the puzzle here and there, and sometimes the answers conflicted with others. I talked with Paul E. the most since we had good rapport, and Paul told me the story about Jesus, who is God, who came to Earth in human flesh to make Him known and to reconcile with people. It was the first time I heard this, but it did not resonate with me, and the idea that an ancient book has all the truth despite contrary findings of modern science was clearly false to me. Nevertheless, I could tell people here were all serious about the Bible but not ignorant of what is widely taught in schools and universities. I kept asking questions about why the Bible is true, and all the answers I got were not convincing.

The last morning of the retreat, I also questioned Katie, a good-hearted regular member of the English Club, about the validity of the Bible, citing some arguments against it I found on the internet, like fictitious people with only first names. Katie responded that people in the Bible were indeed historical with last names, and the Bible was a collection of many different books. Then Katie pushed in my hand a soft-cover Bible available from the table nearby in an earnest manner that I could not refuse.

Predestination and Started to Believe

Back home, after all the recent experiences and learnings, I realized so strangely the Bible was in my bedroom for the first time in my life. I opened it and read, "*What you have in your hands right now is a supernatural book. The words of this book -the Bible- are not merely human words. Instead, these are God's own words, His own personal revelation of Himself to us....*"

I found it hard to believe, but how could my life end up here where I never expected? I was strongly convinced since my graduate school days that people are predestined in life; if anything, this was a clear sign for me. Suddenly, I had a strange thought, like not of my own: "*Even though you do not believe, choose to believe because you love the friends who believe and want to be with them.*" So, at that moment, I decided to believe, and I wrote down my initials inside the front and back cover of the Bible, planning to read the whole book one day.

The next day, my mind was clear, like going through a reset, and it found the logic it had been looking for. God, who created this universe and all natural laws, is certainly not bound by the laws but is the exception to the laws. Humans, as the most complex living entity known in the universe, can only fully communicate and relate to other humans, not any species or robots, so God becoming a human is the best way to let Himself be known.

The story Paul E. told me about Jesus Christ now made absolute sense. Jesus was a historical legend known by the whole world so greatly that even the calendar was changed because of him, and the story of his life was well preserved throughout history and to the present. Wow! This new realization propelled my soul shattering through the mental prison I was previously in. I felt great joy and liberation, like I was blind and hopeless, but now I could see and was full of hope. I searched the internet for more information about God and Jesus, and the more I read, the more I found it made sense.

During the subsequent English Club event, I eagerly informed my American friends there that I had become a believer. I could tell the genuine joy and pleasure in the faces of Adam, Daniel, and some others when they heard this news from me. However, Paul E. did not show such emotion and asked me to talk about that in a separate meeting.

A few days later, I met with Paul as planned, and after eating some Vietnamese food in a nearby restaurant, we went to talk in the community area of my apartment building. It turned out that Paul was not convinced that I truly believed because the last time we talked during The Weekender, I still believed in natural theories and explanations.

What a 180-degree turn of my belief that now I talked about Jesus with zeal and eagerness to do something about it. But Paul stressed this saying, which only later I would understand, "*Salvation is by grace through faith and not because of works.*" Out of my instinct understanding, I responded that true faith would produce works, and Paul looked up his Bible and read, "*James: faith without works is dead.*" From then on, Paul realized there was indeed a radical change in my belief, and he commented, "*Seek, and you will find.*"

Transition to Forensic Engineering Career

Besides doing structural inspections in my engineering consulting business, I also had small remodeling and commercial structure projects where I used Risa-3D, Excel spreadsheets, and AutoCAD 2007 software, for which I bought a pre-owned standalone license to deliver required structural calculations and drawings. Still, the business was slow, and many prospects did not see value in proper engineering design or did not do business with a foreign identity like mine.

I once inspected a commercial building for a remodeling project near downtown Minneapolis. The prospective customer let me go inside the building, and then he mocked me loudly from outside. After telling him the technical steps and procedures to properly do his project, he showed proper etiquette but later went with a different company. Another time, an owner of a new residential dwelling valued at more than $1 million was unwilling to pay $600 for a separate structural solution he was looking for.

During the weekends, I was still diligently working on recruiting and training new members for my Vanduul Conquerors gaming organization in Star Citizen. Motivated by the game's potential and my ambition to have a powerful fleet of military spaceships, I spent thousands of dollars purchasing future ships and also buying and selling them via a Star Citizen trading thread on reddit.com.

Running out of money, I even borrowed $14,000 via the no-interest balance transfer check offered by Chase Bank to cover my living expenses. During this time, seeing that I could not sustain myself financially, I searched and applied for a Forensic Structural engineer position with a couple of companies, including Unified Investigations and Science Inc. Even though I had California and Minnesota P.E. licenses and was already doing structural inspections of residential and commercial buildings on my own, Unified Investigations and Science Inc. denied my application, citing insufficient experience.

By December 2017, I was interviewed with EFI Global Inc. in the company's local office in Edina by my future boss, Dave, a fire investigator since the early days with the company and a Vietnam War veteran. Dave told me of his life as 17 years old in northern Vietnam, shooting people and people shooting at him during the Vietnam War. After this interview, I got through another phone interview with the company's vice president of engineering, who actually liked my work experience and qualifications, and in the end, I got the job as a Senior Forensic Structural engineer with an $80,000 starting salary and full benefits. It was the highest salary I got thus far that seemed to properly compensate for the level of engineering work required. My compensation package normally would include a company-provided truck for travel, but it was not the case, so I ordered a new 2018 Toyota 4Runner to my specifications to be used for work, and the company reimbursed my mileage. Dave also advised me to go to a Buddhist place in the city, apparently not knowing I had just become a Christian convert, or he likely did not believe Christianity was the only true religion.

Before I started working full-time for EFI Global in February 2018, I finished my last commercial project in time. It was the structural design of metal stairs and ship ladders for Calyxt Office and Laboratory Phase 2, which were manufactured by Camelot Metals Inc., a local business and worthy customer that I had been prospecting for over a year. The EFI Global office in Edina had only one other forensic engineer before hiring me, Tom, who had been with the firm for 17 years and was planning to retire in a year. Dave told me wittingly that working for the company was like working for the government, just goofing around all day. However, Tom had been working a lot of overtime covering Minnesota, Wisconsin, Iowa, Nebraska, South Dakota, and North Dakota. Tom said he was being pushed very hard by the office while making a lot of revenue to subsidize the fire investigators who were jealous of him. Only during the winter because of snow, many forensic works with roof inspections were delayed into spring. I did not yet have my own vehicle and was new to the company, so Tom and I traveled together on the company's truck so that Tom could train and show me along the way.

Short-Lived Connections

It was also after so many years I could not recall that I last attended a Valentine's Day party in February. This one was organized by the U of M Navigators with many people I knew. Since knowing my friends at English Club, I had toned down how I dressed to be simple and genuine, how I truly was at the core. However, I felt excited about this party, and I brought about the best of my dress and attitude, like I would go out to pick up girls in the past. It certainly worked as I looked like the center of attention among some girls I was playing a board game with, and out of nowhere, Kristin came to sit down next to me.

Kristin had been one of the regular Frisbee players, and we had developed some mutual attractions before, but this was a clear sign of her attraction toward me. People at the party also noticed it, and then Jonathan came and whispered something into Kristin's ear that I immediately knew was negative. From then on, I stayed away from Jonathan, and he became increasingly attached to Kristin everywhere she went.

At English Club, knowing that I recently believed, Frank insisted that I shall go to a local church instead, and he recommended Bethlehem Baptist Church (BBC) in downtown Minneapolis, so I went to its Sunday service to check it out and met some people I knew like Ted, Daniel, and Kristen who was also a U of M Navigators member and a regular at English Club. I also went to Sunday service at Hope Community Church (HCC), located next to BBC, where I met many other U of M Cru and Navigators friends. Kristen and I went out to a dog sledding organized by BBC, then went shopping at Costco one time, and it was the only date I had in many years until now. I liked Kristen as she was a pretty, good-hearted, and straightforward girl, so I tried to get together with her a few times, but none worked.

The strange thing was, knowing that I recently believed in Christianity, my father disclosed that he also became a believer in early 2017, the same year I did. He and my stepmother were evangelized by a secret Korean Christian organization in Vietnam called the Church of God, and he had been studying the Bible consistently.

My father pointed out that humans are sinners who crucified God incarnate in the person of Jesus Christ. He also insisted that evolution was not true and there were top scientists who did not believe in evolution. At this time, I agreed with everything my father said, except I still believed in evolution because how else did humans come into existence? However, this was not the first time I got feedback like this, and knowing my father's intellectual capacity, I decided to spend time carefully investigating this matter with all my abilities.

Dissecting Theory of Evolution

The term evolution has been used in different fields, not just in biology, like the evolution of televisions, telephones, shoes, cars, etc. Interestingly, only in biology does evolution mean the natural mechanism that brought a human into being from a different species. The proof was said to be in the fossil records and millions of years of change in successive generations. It was clearly a fallacy. For instance, there were also '*fossil records*' of cars with small changes in each generation over many years, but these cars did not evolve into their new forms. Rather, they were designed with specific intentions via complex calculations, testing and experiments, and then manufactured with precision and synchronizations from the factories by intelligent human minds. How much more complex is a human, who is evidently the source of intelligence, compared to a car yet be a product of a non-intelligent process?

But the glaring ridiculous error of human evolution claim was this: Hasn't evolution been going on for millions of years and still continued, but none of this process could be observed live whatsoever? How and when a non-human species became a human unless the non-human morphed into a human or gave birth to a human? Which one was first, the egg or the chicken, during the evolution process? Where and what are the currently living continuous sub-human forms? And what is the next species human evolving into, and which individual is more human than others by what measure?

Here is an example to illustrate the point: The whole process of a human being born into the world, growing up, maturing, growing old then dying can be found and observed live at any given time for any duration.

In the world we are living in, there exists concurrently a full range of life forms at various stages of the claimed evolution process from bacteria to insect to mammal and human. Are they not continuously evolving right now into their next life forms that any stage and duration of this process can be observed live?

If species are evolving into another species all the time, why can't different species interbreed to produce viable, fertile offspring? Can a car with a half-done engine or wheel survive and thrive, much less a human with a half-done vital organ? Cockroaches and sharks were said to have been living well on Earth for hundreds of millions of years through extreme living conditions. Why the need for the existence of humans? Does life have to be in a certain form to survive and thrive when there exist many flying species, aquatic species, and others with totally different living mechanisms and habitats? It was clear there was no need for a human to form in the first place, and humans did not have many advantageous abilities that other species have, as suggested by the natural selection process to be the fittest at the top of the evolution echelon.

What is insulting to genuine intellectual and scientific minds is that the masses and academics consider evolution as science and fact. The entire modern human civilization is built on only a few good scientific theories, like Newtonian physics, Electromagnetism, Relativity, and Quantum mechanics. These are good because they have rigorous mathematics to follow to predict results with sufficient accuracy so that applications in the real world can be made. Yet these are not absolute truths but the best approximations to truth humans could come up with thus far, as these theories had their limitations and would conflict with each other outside their applicable fields.

In contrast, evolution has none of the mathematics, predictions, or applications in the real world but a glaring fallacy despite all the evidence pointing to its impossibility. There exist species with abilities to not only adapt to the environment but also to completely transform in specific ways just during their lifetimes, like a caterpillar to a butterfly and a tadpole to a frog. But, these physical transformations were not due to millions of years of natural selection but innate in the genetic codes of these species. These species do not morph or give birth to another species.

Growing in Christian Belief

Realizing that God created humans to be like in certain ways for His specific purpose was a milestone in my new belief system and more wonder in how I lived my new life. Seemed like a coincidence after my father said a believer shall get baptized. I came to an HCC's Sunday service in March 2018, and it was a baptism day! It also seemed like a coincidence that the senior pastor, who I later knew as Steve, was unusually keen about my presence in the sanctuary as he riveted his sight on me. I signed up excitedly for baptism, and after answering some screening questions from an elder, I came onto the sanctuary stage as the last person to be baptized. I got inside the casket with my whole body submerged in the water except my head. Then suddenly, pastor Steve asked loudly, "*Will you obey Jesus' commandments?*" I never expected and did not understand why I was asked this question. I believed Jesus was God incarnate, and was that all the belief about? But I wanted to be baptized, and if God had commandments for me, then I would obey, so I said "*Yes*" and went full head down into the water.

It was unusually refreshing after I got baptized, and pastor Steve was very nice to see me after to ask some questions. What I also never expected was that Josh L. and his close friend Emma came to see me backstage with great joy, and we exchanged phone numbers like a special relationship was formed. Katelyn was also an HCC member, and she later congratulated me, knowing that I had believed and made it public. What's more, I previously had difficulty believing in the resurrection of Jesus from His death. But with the miraculous refreshing of my mind after being baptized, suddenly the resurrection made perfect sense, and it actually must have happened and surely happened as God's demonstration of His power over life and death precisely to the contrary of any natural laws that were created and controlled by God. Super excited about this mind-blowing realization, I went to my Facebook page and made a reference link to a post I found over the internet called '*15 Logical Reasons to Believe in the Resurrection.*' This post was later mysteriously made erroneous for viewing, apparently being censored for religious content, then eventually was restored.

In April 2018, Sedgwick Claims Management Services, Inc. acquired Cunningham Linsey and its subsidiaries, which included my company, EFI Global. Snow on the roofs melted, and Tom and I got increasingly busy with work. We frequently traveled out of state and stayed overnight in different motels or inns. Tom taught me that it was expensive to be poor, and this also explained what Nathan told me, "*The rich get richer*" while we were still working at Merrill Lynch. Despite reading the Bible several times, Tom confessed he previously could not believe, but after a serious trial in his life, the moral lesson convinced him of the truth. But he believed in evolution with fossil records as proof. I explained to him what I found wrong about evolution, but it did not convince him.

Exploring a Different Church

During these times, after two years, The Rosen Law Firm, P.A. sent me a claim form for Natural Health Trends Corp. Sec. Litig., No. 2:16-cv-00255-TJH-AFM, to review near the end of January 2018. I found various errors in the document, including a typo in the Option Purchase price, Social Security Number (SSN) was used but shall be Taxpayer Identification Number (TIN) for corporate identity, misspellings of my name on the Purchase page that I had to correct them all and send back and forth several times for over one month's length. In early April 2018, I was informed that the judge approved the settlement, including a $3,000 payment for my time as a plaintiff, which I did receive shortly after, but the final claim and total payment for my options would only be finalized about eight months later.

At home, I was still searching and reading more information about God over the internet, which led me to the website of The Church of Jesus Christ of Latter-day Saints (LDS), where I signed up for connection and was mailed some flyers and the Book of Mormon. Soon after, two local LDS missionaries contacted me, and then we met in person at the pizza shop by my apartment building. I was very impressed with the two missionaries, full of peace, joy, and knowledge about God.

By May 2018, I got my new Toyota 4Runner and started to travel and work independently from Tom. Since I got two vehicles, I let some friends at English Club borrow my Toyota Celica as needed.

Persuaded by the LDS missionaries, I decided to attend one of the local LDS temples located in New Brighton, not far from where I lived. The first thing I noticed inside the LDS temple was a painting portrait of Jesus as a white man with blonde hair, which I knew was not true of His ethnicity. I also noticed there was no symbol of the cross, and the missionaries explained that they did not use the symbol of crucifixion and death since Jesus had risen from the dead. They also stated that, unlike other mainstream churches, there was no dealing or collecting money, as Jesus led an example of destroying all the money dealers in the temple. What I found strange was the missionaries' teaching about the baptism of the dead, there were three different levels of heaven to achieve depending on what the believers did on Earth, and only a few really evil people insisting on rejecting God went to hell after being given a second chance on judgment day. I was also taught that the LDS Church president was a living prophet receiving ongoing revelations from God that all members must obey.

I talked to various Christian friends I knew about my recent connection with the LDS church, and they all opposed it. Adam said the LDS church was a counterfeit of the true church of God, and Paul E. said the LDS founder, Joseph Smith, was a fraud. I knew Adam and Paul E. were trustworthy men and took their feedback seriously. I searched the internet for negative information about Joseph Smith and the Book of Mormon and I was convinced that the immoral life of Joseph, the artificial nature of his book, and the race discrimination in LDS church history were true. I still had my affection for the LDS missionaries as I believed they were genuine in their belief, but unfortunately was misled, so I visited the LDS church service one last time to say goodbye. There, I saw the church singing an ancient hymn about Israel, heavily concerned and involved in American politics, and had a number of people called "elect" to stand up and vote for different matters.

Investigating Scientific Assumptions

So far, I had only read the first few chapters of Genesis and John (as recommended by some Christian friends) of the Bible with difficulty absorbing the information. I saw how dense and so much to read the Bible is, and I had no motivation or time allocated to read it further. I saw a post on Facebook from a Christian friend celebrating the six-day creation of the universe, which I found incredibly hard to believe. Then I realized that is what Genesis teaches, and I had trusted what was taught in school that it took many billions of years for the universe and the earth to form as the truth instead of investigating this matter myself. So, at home, I watched a YouTube channel of Kent Hovind, who taught high-school science and math for 15 years. Kent showed that the radiocarbon dating method is based on a number of assumptions, including the constant decay rate, no contamination, and conditions at Time Zero. This was an idealization by which scientific models assume facts about the phenomenon being modeled that are strictly false in reality but make models easier to understand or solve.

Kent also pointed out narratives, which were without any evidence of their existence, presented as facts in high-school science textbooks like The Primordial Soup, where nonliving matter first became living organisms. This idea was disproved following experiments conducted in 1668 by Italian physician Francesco Redi and in 1859 by French chemist and microbiologist Louis Pasteur. I also found a video showing Richard Dawkins, the prominent living atheist and evolutionary biologist, when asked in an interview about the origin of life on Earth, answered that it was from the aliens.

In a documentary film called '*Is Genesis History?*', the speaker showed a canyon with rocks dated from 350 thousand to 2 million years old by radiocarbon method but, in reality, were quickly formed during the volcanic eruption in 1980 at Mount Saint Helens. The radiocarbon dating method gives an extremely wide range of estimates depending on specific assumptions, and there was a commitment to the millions-year paradigm from the mainstream scientific community to fit with the evolution paradigm. A series of Ph.D. scientists in different fields were interviewed and gave convincing explanations supporting a very-young-age Earth, sometimes with evidence like dinosaurs' soft tissue and red blood cells found in its fossil.

Since I had a new realization about how God created the first human, Adam, and then his wife, Eve, and how sins entered the world through them, I found more and more proclaimed Christians actually believed in something else. Their belief ranged from the creation account described in Genesis of the Bible was still going on after billions of years, to evolution as the actual method God used to create humans. I strongly opposed these beliefs because realizing the nature of human sins was of supreme importance, and these beliefs left no legitimacy for sins and the crucifixion of Jesus.

Exploring Bible Study Groups

One day, I went to a Bible study session at the Cru building in Dinkytown led by Dakota; another attendant was an African international student. After hearing my literal interpretation of the Scriptures, the student commented that the Bible was not a science textbook, it was spiritual only, and I was the first one he had ever met with a literal interpretation.

Surprisingly, Dakota also stated that he saw evolution all the time as he was majoring in Microbiology and that he still believed there was a God. Disappointed inside, I figured I could not explain myself nor convince the two otherwise at that moment, so I commented with a Bible verse I had heard before: "*For the gate is narrow and the way is hard that leads to life, and those who find it are few.*"

During this time, I attended some more One Church events where I talked to Jenna about the progress in my belief and how I no longer thought Jesus was a prophet, but God came on earth to save humans. Jenna also shared that she found peace from believing in Jesus regardless of life's circumstances, which I had not heard about before and seemed like a powerful state of being.

My conversations with other people also made a lot more sense than in the past, but still, there were many things new to me. I also met Connor, who was very pleasant and seemed unusually mature in his Jesus-like character. Connor invited everyone to the summer Bible study course at the Cru building, so I attended. I was very impressed with Connor's moral story of a frog trying to fly but eventually realized and became content with what God meant for it. During a prayer-walking routine around the area after a Bible study session, Connor also puzzled me by telling everyone with confidence that if someone was very spiritual, then impossible miraculous things would occur.

On the 4th of July 2018, I gave Matt a ride to the National Sports Center complex in Blaine to play sports and watch fireworks with Cru's summer Bible study group. Matt was also a chemical engineering student at the U of M like Ted but hung out with both the Navigators and Cru, like me. Everyone played wiffle ball, which I did not know, so I brought my soccer ball and kicked it around. After a while, some people started playing a World Cup soccer game with me, and later, Gabriel was very nice to keep passing the ball from the corner for me to practice heading. When everyone was resting after all the activities, I was still practicing shooting, and I was disappointed that my power was weak. Suddenly, a strange spirit of determination rushed on me, and I kicked the ball from outside the box area. The ball was driven about three times more powerful than my last shot, and I could not believe my eyes. It hit both goalposts in succession, then it bounced off near Connor, and he passed the ball back to me. I tried the shot again, expecting my new power, but it was weak like before, and I could not understand why.

Also, during that month, Unified Investigations and Sciences, which previously denied my job application, was joining my company to operate under the brand name EFI Global.

In August 2018, I moved to live in a one-bedroom at Saint Anthony Village Apartments at 519 3rd Avenue Southeast, where I still live up to the present. Since then and in subsequent months, my work got busier; I had to travel out of state and stay overnight frequently and missed the rest of the Bible study course.

Later, I was somehow invited via Facebook to a party in a big house organized by U of M Cru students, most of whom I knew. I had a number of reports to write for my recent forensic inspections, but I did not want to miss the party, so I brought my laptop with me to work there also. People were preparing the food at the house when I came, so I sat down and worked on my laptop at the table on the front porch where Josh L. and others were also waiting. Then I saw Dakota, and he was not happy seeing me. He informed me that my invitation was a mistake and I was not supposed to be there, so I left and felt sad as I rarely had any house parties in the first place. Later, at an HCC's Sunday service, Josh L. told me I should have stayed that day at the party, and I appreciated his compassion.

Experiences That Changed People

Next, in my mind, the concepts of heaven and hell I heard from the Bible were difficult to digest and understand, so I kept watching YouTube videos about these topics. I found videos in which medical doctors discussed a known phenomenon called near-death experiences (NDEs). NDEs include out-of-body experiences, pleasant feelings, seeing deceased relatives, a life review, or a conscious return to the body. Patients who have been through an NDE showed significant transformation in their spiritual and emotional lives, with many stating a renewed sense of meaning, existential awareness, and mystical experiences.

Eben Alexander, an adopted child and a neurosurgeon who had taught at Harvard Medical School, described his experience while suffering from bacterial meningitis to his entire brain and in a coma for 7 days. He saw gorgeous and ultra-real details of greenery, trees, and butterflies and felt a warm, divine breeze and love. Eben also met a young woman he did not know and connected with her nonverbally. After miraculously recovering to tell the story, he was sent a photo of his biological sister, who died before they ever met, and she was exactly that woman. Eben totally changed his previous views of materially based reality to become a true believer in a personal and loving God after the experience.

I also watched video testimony of some people attesting to their experiences of hell. Howard Storm, a former atheist and professor at Northern Kentucky University, described in an emotionally charged way his experience when he was suddenly diagnosed with duodenal perforation and passed out. Subsequently, he was looking at his body, his wife, and his roommate from a third-person view, and there were 'people' calling him outside of the room. He went with them while he could not believe what was happening; everything was hyper-reality. After a very long journey of ever-increasing closeness and darkness, he became really scared, resisted, and fought these 'people.' There were a lot of them who were completely devoid of love, hope, and good. They could annihilate him, but they were interested in tormenting and morally debasing him in exquisite ways that the physical pains were not measured up to the psychological and emotional pains. Desperate for escape, he recalled and sang a song he was taught and believed in when he was a little kid, "*Jesus loves me, that I know,*" that eventually brought him back from the out-of-body experience. Since then, Howard has become a devout believer and serves as a pastor in his church.

Another Fall Retreat and Weekender

In October 2018, I put aside some work and used paid time off to attend Cru Fall Retreat and Navigators Weekender. I also volunteered as a driver since my Toyota 4Runner was a very good road trip vehicle with plenty of space for passengers and luggage. I met mostly the same Christian friends, was familiar with how things went, and was active in learning scriptures and group discussions this time, and nothing unexpected happened during the Cru Retreat.

However, during the first large group greeting of the Navigators Weekender, I noticed the speaker was unusually spirit-driven and spoke loudly and repeatedly that anyone was welcome there, regardless of whether the person was a virgin or promiscuous, or interested in attractive young girls there; but you must come as who you are, and no '*diet coke Jesus.*' I could tell my presence at this place raised some eyebrows, and he was talking about me. I appreciated that he publicly announced the welcome, which made me feel more secure.

The next day, near the end of lunchtime, there was a very senior-looking staff member whom I did not know came and sat at my table, and we talked. I fervently told him I was taught nothing else except evolution, but through digging and examining various related sciences, evolution was clearly impossible and never happened, yet many professing Christians believe in it. I also claimed I had examined evidence pointing to the existence of heaven and hell, then a sudden spirit rushed on me, and I could not believe that I said the Bible shall be interpreted literally (as I really had not read it yet).

However, the senior staff seemed to disagree, saying that God does whatever he wants at any time. I immediately rebuked him: not to have the wrong understanding to corrupt God's words. He nodded, acknowledging what I said, but I sensed it was only superficial, and he did not have genuine affection for God and His unchangeable words.

Once again, a sudden spirit rushed on me, and I could not believe that I exclaimed God knew all the hidden things and was witnessing this very conversation. I thanked God for revealing the truth to me despite all the world's deceptions, and then I looked at the senior staff member with stern, scrutinizing eyes. Then he stood up and left, and I realized everyone in the building had left.

I continued learning new things during the Weekender by discussing different religious topics. Josh Y., a regular at the English Club and architecture student at the U of M, shared with me that he had changed from the inside for the better after learning about God's character. He told me what I had not heard before: God first pursues lost people, and then these people pursue God.

I was also very impressed with Josh B. as the speaker at the seminar about the sovereignty of God. He was the assistant to the U of M Navigators' Campus Director, Trevor L., whom together I thought were father and son, full of peace and joy when I first met them.

What I learned from the seminar and subsequent discussion was that human free will is a complex and difficult topic. Previously, I was firmly convinced that there was no free will, but if that were true, how just and loving is it that so many people were destined to be sent to hell by God? Therefore, I was inclined to believe humans were responsible in certain ways. Also, there was a seminar I attended about the Navigators' 20s in the Twin Cities. I signed up for the Navigators' 20s at the end of the seminar, but I never heard back from them.

Getting Involved Religiously

After the Weekender, I attended the U of M Navigators' weekly meeting on Thursday nights organized at Sojourn Campus Church as often as my work schedule allowed. A typical night included singing worship songs, listening to a speaker on a topic, discussions in small groups, and socializing at the end.

I knew all of the Navigators' staff and many students at these meetings, and Josh B. advised me that I should trust the Bible, to which I agreed in principle but still had not really read it yet. I was aware that these meetings were for U of M students, which I was not, so I asked Ted if I should come, to see if I got any support. Ted taught me that God is good and said I should come.

One day after the meeting, I noticed a wooden cross had been a long-standing fixture near the side windows, and then I felt unusually merry that I stood up and leaned my back along the cross with my arms stretched out like I was being crucified. Christine, standing nearby, saw what I was doing and looked at me weirdly, so I stopped doing it.

On and off, I attended Sunday services at HCC and BBC in downtown Minneapolis, participating in worship, singing, and listening to sermons. Most of the time, I just sat by myself, but one day, when I came to the upper level of HCC's sanctuary, I saw Khiara, a U of M student who also attended English Club, sitting by herself. So I sat next to her, and we talked. We knew each other quite well and were developing a connection, as she previously warned me of going to LDS church. The next Sunday, I came to the same spot expecting to talk to her again, but I saw Andrew, a U of M Cru member, already sitting next to her, preventing me from doing so. Andrew had always been sitting with his friends on the other side of the upper level, and clearly, he went out of his way to do this. Andrew and I also knew each other as we both attended the previous Fall Retreats and discussed theology since my early days when I knew next to nothing about Christianity. It was after he found out about my old age that I could tell his attitude changed toward me.

I also attended some swing dance classes in the evening and came to the Ukrainian American Community Center for practice. Just by chance, I met and talked briefly at the Center with Meg, a U of M Navigators member, who previously taught me and others some swing dance moves during a Navigators party. Then suddenly, this stranger approached, and I could tell he likely was Meg's boyfriend, so I left them alone. Not long after that, I went out on a weekend night to the rooftop of Stella's Fish

Café in Uptown Minneapolis to get refreshed. It had been a very long time since I last went out to a night spot, so I did not talk to any girls at all and was just chilling. Then I saw Meg's boyfriend was also hanging out there but without her. What I did not expect was that the guy came and stood in front of me, showing his back and blocking my view intentionally. I had experienced many cock blockings of all sorts during my earlier years of going out, but this one without any girl physically around was the first of its kind.

In November 2018, I was informed that Dan, the Campus Outreach leader and a regular at the English Club, fell seriously ill and had to be hospitalized because of his cancer, even though he had been under chemo and radiation therapy treatment for a while. The last time I saw him with his wife and children, he had lost so much weight that it was striking. In his last message to friends that I knew when he was staying in the hospital, he asked everyone to pray for him. Dan was a good-hearted leader; I liked him a lot and wanted his company. So, I prayed earnestly to God that he would recover. It was the first time I prayed for someone and believed God definitely answers and saves such a good believer. But Dan died shortly after that to my disbelief. Then I attended the celebration of his life at BBC in downtown Minneapolis and wondered why God let this happen.

At home, I found a free movie on YouTube called '*Jesus of Nazareth,*' totaling more than 6 hours in length that was made in 1977. I was unusually absorbed in the movie and watched it several times over several months, and I still watch it to this very day. Whenever I watched Jesus performing a miracle of healing, comforting, forgiving, and saving various miserable and dead people, I cried deeply in a way I was not capable of in the past. Impressed in my mind was a scene of Jesus talking with the religious leader Joseph of Arimathea; the greatest commandment was "*Thou shalt love the Lord thy God with all thy heart, with all thy soul, with all thy strength,*" and the second commandment no less great was "*You must love your neighbor as yourself.*" Impressed in my mind was another scene in the temple, a group of religious professionals seeing a born blind person had miraculously gotten his sight back but denied it by saying he pretended to be blind to earn his living in front of Jesus and everyone. Jesus said to them, "*I came into this world to give sight to those who cannot see and to take away sight from those who can. If you were blind, you would be without sin, but since you say we see, your sin remains.*"

By March 2019, while I was on a long road trip back from an inspection assignment, I turned on the local radio in my Toyota 4Runner and heard this song that filled me with extreme emotion, and I cried deeply through the rest of the trip. The song sang, "*We believe in God the Father. We believe in Jesus Christ. We believe in the Holy Spirit. And He's giving us new life. We believe in the crucifixion. We believe that He conquered death. We believe in the resurrection. And He's coming back again, we believe.*" Knowing the song was inspired by God with absolute certainty, when I got back home, I looked up the lyrics on the internet and found the song name was '*We Believe,*' composed and performed by the Newsboys band. Since then, I have listened to this song many times, and it has become my personal single worship song.

The Unexpected

During the winter of 2019, there was significantly more snow than that of an average year in Minnesota and Wisconsin. And I had a number of inspections for snow damage to roof structures. Some of these damages were legitimately due to the actual snow load exceeded the design snow load, but that was not the case for the rest of the damage claims. From an inspection for snow damage to a large barn's roof structure, I found the wood truss members to be quite smaller than normally expected. Yet the builder claimed that these trusses were engineered to resist the design snow load. Because the barn was built not too long ago, the owner had the construction drawing, and I used my Risa-3D program to model and analyze the truss under an unbalanced snow load as required by building codes. The analysis results showed that, indeed, the wood truss was significantly undersized and failed under the required design snow load. My boss, Dave, told me that the builder objected to my findings, and I might be prepared to testify in court. However, the builder never provided any evidence that the wood truss was designed by a licensed engineer, and the case closed.

In April 2019, Tom, my only forensic structural engineer colleague in the office, retired. Previously, there was a time period of peak workload crisis for which I needed my boss, Dave, but seemingly coincidently, he was on vacation and did not respond to any communication. This time, I asked Dave if a new engineer was hired in place of Tom as previously planned, but Dave informed me bluntly that he could not hire anyone for various reasons, like one was supposed to take the job but changed his mind. Subsequently, the workload previously for two engineers was all assigned to my name. I got close to 30 inspection assignments, including out-of-state travel, staying overnight, and corresponding reports to complete in 2 weeks. When I planned them on a time schedule, I would have to literally work around the clock to make it. Fortunately for me, in a way, as the parent company Sedgwick kept continuously acquiring other companies and consolidating them under its corporate umbrella, my local office needed to start conforming to Chicago's EFI Global office, and my workload was relieved to a more manageable level for me.

Near the end of May 2019, I was informed that Terri, a lovely middle-aged lady and one of the two office administrative assistants in my local office, fell ill quickly and died from ovarian cancer. I was shocked since

I last met her at Tom's retirement party and heard that her chemo and radiation therapy were making progress. I came to Terri's memorial service at Peace Lutheran Church in Robbinsdale along with other people in my company and was told that she lost weight very quickly and then faded away. A pattern emerged in my mind that Dan and Terri, in their middle age and good-hearted believers, got cancer the last few years and went through chemo and radiation therapy, but both lost weight quickly and then passed away. Recalling the various failures of modern doctors and the great success of natural leaves and herbs many years ago in treating the terminal illness of my paternal grandmother, who is still living this very day in her 90+, I was convinced chemo and radiation therapy hurts a lot more than helps the patients and was just another means of making money for the medical industry.

Also, at this time, more than one year after the judge approved the settlement of my claim for NHTC Securities Litigation, I was contacted by Strategic Claims Services, a third-party company. I was informed that the pro-rata distribution for the settlement was $0.02558 per dollar of each authorized claimant's recognized loss. The pro-rata payout for my claim, #42, is $1,474.02, which was extremely small compared to my total loss. I asked how this $0.02558 per dollar was determined as I had seen in some documents $0.20 per dollar after legal fees. The answer I got was, "*The recovery listed in the Notice was an estimate, not the dollar amount of the actual recovery. The pro-rata is only known once all claims in the case have been processed.*" The recognized loss for my claim was only $57,622.50; apparently, the majority of my loss was forced liquidations and was not recognized. Then I asked how much the legal fee was but never got a reply.

By July 2019, I had obtained P.E. licenses in 11 states as required and recommended by my boss, including Texas, Florida, and New York which I started applying for since 2013 and eventually submitted all the

New York state-specific paper-based forms. However, I was still denied by the North Dakota State Board because my bachelor's degree is not ABET-accredited. I need to have double the qualifying experience of someone with an ABET-accredited bachelor's degree. My master's degree from the State University of New York at Buffalo and the fact that my bachelor's degree meets the NCEES Engineering Education Standard do not help in this matter. Also, to be considered for the work experience with my company, TATran Corp, I needed to provide, in great detail, the actual principles and specialized engineering education I applied to these projects. I was informed that, in addition to more detailed descriptions, any work product or examples of my work would be beneficial to the North Dakota State Board.

During these times, I was extremely busy with work, traveling out of state, staying overnight often, and working in the evenings and on weekends. On one occasion, I was on the road for three consecutive days, accumulating more than 1500 miles. I gave up running my gaming organization, Vanduul Conquerors, during the weekends for a month, and a number of members left and trashed our Discord server. Subsequently, I had to clean it up then minimize my involvement time with the organization.

As compensation for my work, I got a small salary raise a couple of times to more than $84,000 and started getting quarterly bonuses, the 2nd quarter bonus was more than $14,000, and the 3rd quarter bonus was almost $40,000. After a while, I got burnt out and had pains in my lower back and legs and had to go through physical therapy but did not have time to complete the treatment. Fortunately, my boss, Dave, retired early, and my local office was fully under the direction of my new bosses, Ron, the Midwest district manager, and Carl, the principal engineer in Chicago's EFI Global office. Both Ron and Carl showed more understanding and provided me with temporary help as needed, but I was still the only structural forensic engineer in my local office.

Where Do I Fit In?

On one Thursday night, I came to the U of M Navigators' weekly meeting at Sojourn Campus Church and the students had to check in and their name tags were printed from a list. I felt out of place because it was a new school year with many new faces, and I saw Trevor L., the Campus Director, standing inside the entrance. So I quietly reaffirmed my impression with him that this was not for me, and I was about to leave. But surprisingly, Trevor smiled big, then printed out my name from the list and affixed the name tag on my shirt. And with this approval from Trevor, I came as often as my work schedule allowed. I also recalled Paul R., whom I met at English Club for over a year and who had invited me over to his house the previous Thanksgiving, strongly recommended that I read through the whole Bible via a plan on my cell phone, so I installed a Bible study application and started using it while having meals on my work trips. Paul R. was previously a police officer but left his job to found and lead Risen Church in Minneapolis.

In October 2019, for the third year in a row, I put aside some work and attended both Cru Fall Retreat and Navigators Weekender as they were my primary social reliefs of the year. I still volunteered as a driver, and nothing unexpected happened except more than half of the people I knew in the past had graduated or would be graduating that year. There were Navigators' staff who considered me an old driver, as Adam wittingly called me so. I never told anyone my age, and I fit in well with the students, likely because of my young appearance and little social understanding. I wondered how the staff knew my age and how old they were if they considered me old. Also, at the beginning of a group photo taking, I was physically pushed away by one of the students whom I did not see. Apparently, the retreat and appearance in photos were meant for young people only.

During another U of M Navigators night, I came across Trevor L. while on my way in, and he smilingly asked me, "*What is your motivation for coming here?*" I recalled a related Bible verse and answered him, "*In order to have a fulfilled life,*" then I showed him the Bible study application on my phone and quoted some verses I was reading: "*These people left our churches, but they never really belonged with us; otherwise, they would have stayed with us. When they left, it proved that they did not belong with us.*" At that time, I neither knew the context nor fully understood the meaning of these verses, but strangely, I felt these verses were telling me that on paper and appearance, I was the outsider, but in truth, I was the minority insider. After hearing the verses, Trevor signaled me to come in, and as I understood it, he meant the majority of students here had not known the things of God. Trevor did not always come to the Navigators night, but I noticed that sometimes he joined group discussions with the students as I did. I understood this as Trevor showed an example to support my unusual involvement with the students.

Around these times at English Club, at the beginning of a meeting, when I got in the line for a free meal as always, I saw Frank sitting at a nearby table, and surrounding him were Noah, Adam, and other believers. Both Frank's eyes were strangely scary red. I never saw him like that, and from the look of things, it seemed like the friends had to surround Frank to soothe and talk him out of something. I recalled the same kind of red eyes I had seen from some previous jealous and spiteful members of my gaming organization that I expelled, so I prepared my mind for a heated opposition to my presence from Frank. But unexpectedly, Frank seemed to read what I was thinking and said, "*Tony, you are welcome here to eat the food, and you can also take home as much as you want.*" Up until the present, that was the only time I saw Frank with red eyes, and since then, he no longer had any hostility toward me.

Attacked by Satan and Rescued by the Holy Spirit

Still Pursuing the Worldly

My job kept me busy all the way till the end of 2019, so I did not take any vacation time, and my 4th quarter bonus was more than $25,000. I had been making enough money to pay off my previous debt with Chase Bank, pay off my Toyota 4Runner loan, and accumulate savings. I also had been giving small monthly donations to some Navigators staff. Because of snow accumulating on the roofs, my job slowed down during early 2020, and I had time to attend a Winter Retreat with the U of M Navigators for the first time. For the first time, I also attended additional weekly Monday nights with the U of M Navigators called '*Equip,*' where scripture memorizing was the emphasis. During an Equip night, when people were divided up into small groups for discussion, I was hesitant to join groups with girls, but unexpectedly, Josh B., who was the organizing staff, directed me to join a group with girls. Later, Josh also encouraged me to join any group I would like and told me there was no exclusivity or segregation here like in some other places.

Interestingly, also attending Equip nights was Mason, Meg's boyfriend. I noticed Mason had been coming to various U of M Navigators meetings with and without Meg, and he certainly noticed me, too. We were in a group chat a few times before and eventually had a conversation between us. Mason's attitude toward me had changed to a polite and pleasant one; apparently, because of the social setting we were in, I was not a total stranger. In our conversation, I found out that Mason was serving in the U.S. military and would soon become a sergeant. As I had been training members in my gaming organization for disciplines and spaceship combat skills regularly for several years, I expressed an interest in serving and training in the U.S. military if I were a young American. Mason told me that one can still join the military for the first time up to the age of 35, but I replied that, unfortunately, I had passed that age limit, and he was surprised because I did not look that old. At the end of our conversation, I appreciated Mason's service to the country, and that was the last time we met.

During this time, I managed to write in great detail the actual principles and specialized engineering education I applied to the projects with my own company in the past. In addition, I also provided examples of my actual work as recommended and sent to the North Dakota State Board as required for my P.E. application. After sending all these documents, I checked with the Board, and they confirmed that they had received everything and scanned the documents. However, since then, I have neither received a reply from them nor approval of my P.E. application with the Board until this very day.

After an English Club meeting near the end of February 2020, Adam and I got into a private talk – just the two of us. Adam asked me about the progression in my faith, and I honestly told him I was still pursuing my original American dream of one day becoming rich with a trophy girlfriend or wife, along with otherworldly things. I also told him about the Barna Group's research I read, showing the 10-stop journey of a Christian transformation to the ultimate stage of wholeness and maturity. The research showed most Americans never get beyond Stop 3, which was awareness and concern about sin and its effects. And among those who become '*born again Christians,*' most never move past Stop 5, which was having invited Christ to be their savior and then engaging in a lot of religious activity. Barna also determined that most church programs are designed to help people get to Stop 5 of the journey but not to move farther down the road to Christ-likeness. I did not see why I should be any different from an average American believer.

In the back of my mind, I acknowledged with Adam that truly following God is like selling everything to buy the land with ultimate hidden treasure as described in a parable of the Bible. I also acknowledged that God's value system is true and best for humans, but we were too foolish to recognize it. Knowing that, however, I still wanted and pursued the world's value system as it was all I had been doing for many years, and it had powerful attachments and appeal to it.

Adam responded by telling me about his experience working with guys who could not get a girlfriend and got stuck watching pornography and masturbating. I felt like he was indirectly talking about me, but I did not see how watching pornography and masturbating was wrong or a sin because it did not actually affect any other person and also helped to relieve stress. Adam concluded our private talk with a long and serious prayer that God will empower me to overcome all the obstacles so that I will fully submit and follow God.

Creators and Creations

In March 2020, COVID-19 was declared a global pandemic and national emergency in the U.S. Subsequently, people were ordered to stay home, and all social gatherings and activities were shut down. Fortunately, my job involved very little social interaction and was only slightly affected by the pandemic. Nevertheless, my company decided to freeze all salary raises and stopped contributions to employees' retirement plans.

Staying at home and not going anywhere except traveling for work, I had more time to watch various apologetic and religious videos on YouTube, and I stopped using the Bible study application on my phone. On the weekends, I continued to recruit and train members in my gaming organization and broadcasted live regularly on our YouTube channel, Vanduul Conquerors. The vast majority of players were young and severely lacking in discipline, and the turnover of new members was very high as they gave up training. I also continuously spent a lot of money on acquiring a fleet of powerful military spaceships in the game. These activities were where I got satisfaction from my ego and pride as someone totally in charge.

Up until the present, Star Citizen was still in alpha development, underwent multiple technical breakthroughs and expansions in scope, and had an unknowable release date to be the most realistic and greatest space simulation ever. Through the development years of the game, I saw an uncanny parallel to the creation story in the Bible. Everything in the game was designed and created organically to all the little details, from human characters, aliens, items, spaceships, planets, cities, physics for all the interactions in the atmosphere and in space, etc. When I want a ship of mine to be in the game, my character just needs to select that ship and click a button on a space station computer, and the ship, no matter its size or complexity, instantly appears out of nothing in the game universe at the designated location. There were many different ships with various sizes, styles, functionalities, and intended purposes. But the ship designer was the sole reason why a ship was the way it was, not because of requirements or selection mechanisms from the game environment. Some ships were good for their purposes, and some were bad. Some were made just because it was a cool-looking or unique design, etc.

According to the Big Bang theory, the prevailing cosmological model explaining the existence of the observable universe from the earliest known periods, from a singularity without space and time, all matter and energy in the whole universe came into existence instantly. At around the 10^{-32} seconds mark from the beginning, the universe's volume had already increased by a factor of at least 10^{78}, which meant the bulk of the present universe was also formed instantly. Only when back-calculating using specific assumptions about the universe's expansion rate was the universe's age determined to be around 14 billion years. What was significant was that according to modern scientists in this field, during the beginning time of the universe, the present physical laws did not apply. Also, the vast majority of gravitational effects and gravitational potential in the universe were recently found to be not from primordial building materials and were not created by baryonic matter, but were essentially from non-physical and invisible things, called dark matter and dark energy.

Watching YouTube, I came across a video presentation of the mathematical Mandelbrot Set from Dr. Jason Lisle of the Biblical Science Institute. The Set was very complex, and when it was computationally graphed on a computer screen, it showed a fascinating fractal that seemingly had various figures of the world we live in at any scale. I recalled Einstein’s theory of relativity proposing that time was essentially another dimension of space woven together into the unified fabric of space-time continuity. This space-time continuum was supported to be true by many experiments to test its validity over the years and had real-world applications like in the Global Positioning System (GPS). If fractal patterns were how God created many things in the world as readily observable, and time was indeed another space dimension, then fractal patterns shall be observable throughout history also. This means there were patterns of things that occurred in the past that shall repeatedly occur in the future at various time intervals, and predestination was true.

However, according to scientists in the field of quantum mechanics, things operate in very weird, logic-defying ways at the scale of atoms and subatomic particles. The state of a quantum particle is intrinsically indeterministic, conforms to a precise probability distribution, and does not exist until it is measured. Quantum entanglement is the phenomenon Einstein never believed to be true and described as a '*spooky action at a distance*' when two or more particles link up in a certain way; no matter how far apart they are in space, their states remain linked. And any action to one of these particles will instantly impact the other particles, measurably faster than the speed of light. Various stringent experiments made possible by recent technology with mathematical rigor have proved these to be true, and quantum mechanics had many real-world applications, like the laser and the computer transistor. I saw all of the above as evidence that there was infinitely more than a human can understand about the nature of the world that God created. If humans could travel continuously at the speed of light for all generations, it would still cover a meaningless distance compared to the size of the observable universe.

Close But Not Quite

During this time, I watched a series of videos from the Grace Evangelical Society in which Mr. Bob Wilkin, who had a doctorate in theology, taught about God's free salvation through faith alone in Jesus Christ. He argued that God either chose to save humans or not, it was all up to Him and not up to us, which was undeniably true. He went on to present that this saving transaction between God and the sinner is simply the giving and receiving of a free gift. Therefore, he concluded, obedience to the Word of God, while not necessary for obtaining everlasting life, is the essential responsibility of each Christian. It is inconsistent with the gospel and scriptures to seek to gain or keep everlasting life by godly living. The scriptures, however, do present several motivations for obedience in the Christian life. I was convinced that his points were true and felt relieved as a believer. However, I also felt it would be easy to be saved and that there would be no passion for God or a strong connection with God like that of other things in life.

Subsequently, I watched a very interesting video series called '*Closer to Truth,*' in which Mr. Robert Lawrence Kuhn, who had a doctorate in neuroscience and was a long-time advisor to the Chinese government, interviewed various experts in a very wide range of fields from philosophy, science, theology, etc. to find answers for difficult questions regarding the cosmos, consciousness, and God. The experts indeed found many insights; however, no one truly knew the nature of consciousness and the unified self of a person despite physical changes over time in the body and the brain. I saw that Mr. Kuhn had obtained a well of knowledge pointing to an intelligent and all-powerful creator, but ironically, he still could not come to the knowledge of the truth about God. In his interview with a philosopher of religion, the expert said that a person needs a religious experience in order to believe in God, which I had never heard about, and I did not understand what it is and why it is so. Apparently, I and many others believe in God without having a religious experience.

In May 2020, I found all four of my sets of full-length thermal underwear had worn enough over the years that I needed replacement. Normally, I would not purchase them until I actually needed them during the cold winter, but this time, I felt like preparing in advance. However, I could not find the exact replacements, so I searched for different sets online and purchased four sets of full-length white as-snow thermal underwear, fleece lined. I was happy with how they looked and felt in my hands, but I did not try them on and put them in my under-bed storage until the day I needed them.

At work, I had been doing well with my job and developed good connections with the people in the local office and with Carl and Ron in the Chicago office. I also gained good experience as an expert witness from participating in several arbitration meetings. However, at my gaming organization, I realized after years of putting in consistent efforts I made great progress in multi-crew training and procedure but virtually no progress in building up a regular faithful team of players. More or less, a thousand players whom I had personally recruited and trained all went their own ways or betrayed me to join or form other organizations. So, I started to enforce regular participation in team play and gradually expelled the members who did not comply. By July 2020, I had dismissed all inactive members, and my Vanduul Conquerors gaming organization eventually ceased all activities later. I was very sad and disoriented that I had put so much heart and money into this over five years, and it had become a part of who I am but was no more.

Being free from managing my gaming organization during the weekends but restricted from attending any social activity, I watched more videos about God on YouTube. I found videos of some obscure but sincere preachers, listened to their advice, and prayed earnestly in my heart to the Lord Jesus Christ to save me. It was the first time I truly humbled and prayed to God just by myself, and I did it on several occasions.

Independent of Matters

Subsequently, my job got increasingly busy as I was assigned hail damage inspection for a series of residential areas ranging from around

10 to over 25 multi-family buildings each. I performed inspections during the weekdays and wrote most reports during the weekends to keep up with deadlines. Still, there was a lot more work than I could handle, so my company sent an engineer from out of state and not yet licensed in Minnesota to temporarily work with and under my supervision.

My total bonus for the second and third quarters of the year ended up being more than $30,000, but by October 2020, my job's workload had come back down to a normal level. I felt itchy to do something entertaining, so I bought selective computer parts to build a unique liquid-cooling personal computer like I did many years before. For me, it was like a kid building LEGO toys from all the different interlocking parts, and it took a number of trials and errors to be successful. I was also curious about the emerging virtual reality technology and had ordered the latest at that time, a virtual reality headset to be used with the computer. Still, I never stopped seeking more understanding about God. I found myself realizing and moving on from the superficial or bad content to deeper learning materials, including the teaching of R.C. Sproul and John Piper, which were both new to me.

Strikingly was an interview video of Dr. Sam Parnia, who claimed to be not religious and was a physician and professor of medicine at New York University Langone Medical Center, specializing in resuscitation. He confirmed evidence showing the existence of consciousness of some already dead patients for a certain time duration. These were unexplained cases in which the patient did not have any brain activity, yet after coming back to life, they demonstrated intact consciousness and accurately described what was happening in the room during that time. In a video presentation by Dr. Dean Radin, chief scientist at the Institute of Noetic Sciences, new experiments showed consciousness affects matters. These results suggest consciousness was independent of and was the cause of changes in matters. These results directly contradict the currently popular belief and teaching that meaningless materialistic processes brought about everything, including human intelligence and consciousness.

By December 2020, I had accumulated almost a month's worth of paid time off, and my company policy was to take it or lose it each calendar year, so I decided to use them all for the remainder of the year. I got feedback from my manager that even though my time off request was approved, I should still be ready to take '*emergency assignments*' as needed during that time. With some difficulty, I finished building the custom personal computer as I envisioned and tested out the latest virtual reality headset. The liquid cooling system worked very well, but the capability of the computer hardware and virtual reality tech was not as good as advertised by the companies that made them. At the same time, I was still watching sermons by R.C. Sproul, listening to '*Ask Pastor John*' podcasts and John Piper's teachings of the New Testament. Despite being recorded years ago, these explained and clarified the difficult theological issues extremely well.

Strangely, my excitement with the new computer and tech did not last long like it had in the past, and looking to entertain myself, I found a free online erotic adventure game called '*Treasure of Nadia.*' At first, the game appeared to be a simple story of a young man following his father's footsteps, searching for ancient treasures in a town, and hooking up with various women along the way. However, the more I played the game, the more I was hooked by the incredible artwork, twisted storyline, and especially the spiritual elements the game was built on. As the young man progressed in the game, he discovered mysterious forces of evil influencing the people and the world he lived in. At the same time, he gradually acquired various abilities to trample on scorpions, circumvent poisonous snakes, and so on. The game story revealed that cunning and powerful people, by acquiring forbidden treasures, got a curse to age and die, and so did the young man. However, there was hope for a cure that the young man may discover with great difficulty, and I became increasingly more interested in the game's plot rather than its erotic elements.

Breakthrough Spirit

During my paid time off, my company indeed still gave me two new work assignments, and not only that, some of my previously completed assignments came back with additional questions to answer. There were also emails from engineers in other offices I did not know asking for help with their job assignments. One even asked specifically for an engineer with a background in earthquake engineering, which included me. I remember in the yearly performance review, there was a section about teamwork and helping others, in which I was rated low. In the past, while I was very busy, I was asked by an engineer in Texas to unnecessarily make a phone call to talk to a Vietnamese homeowner that was assigned to him; the homeowner spoke English. So, the engineers who were too busy doing their overloaded work were rated low while those who just communicated all day to keep others busy were rated high!

Subsequently, like water reached its boiling temperature; all the pieces of my life puzzle came together, showing the full hidden picture. I realized clearly how I had been killing myself to pursue worthless and harmful things throughout my life. I had been lied to, tempted, and fooled by the world all along the way to serve its own selfish and predatory agenda while believing the sky was the limit I could reach one day. All of these kept me busy working and prevented me from social access and understanding, leading to spiritual and literal death, not knowing God and the truly good things He wants for me. Then, I felt distaste for the lifeless computer hardware and the fake world in video games and virtual reality. I felt distaste for pornography and other adult entertainment as I realized they were the baits to sinful acts against God's design of holy human living. I desired to live according to God's design and goodwill. I desired to work for Him regardless, and it's the only thing that matters. So, I purged everything from my personal computer and stopped playing with it.

Later, I found out that the U of M Navigators recently resumed their weekly Thursday night meeting via Zoom, so I eagerly attended them, like starting a fresh new life. By the end of December, for winter break study, there were different small group topics offered to members also via Zoom, so I selected '*Trusting in God*' and '*VeggieTales,*' even though I did not know what these were about.

In the '*Trusting in God*' group, there was Hanna, the group leader, and Lydia, whom I had known for several years, and other newer members. I never discussed deep religious things with anyone, except recently with Adam, but strangely, I had been studying the same topic on my own. I was so emotionally moved during the discussion that I poured my whole heart out. I exclaimed to the group that the devil was attacking us with his lies and how God had changed my mind and then changed my heart.

In the '*VeggieTales*' group, the only one I knew for several years was Jeremy, the group leader. Jeremy showed a cartoon video about a group of personified veggies traveling through a desert carrying an ark, then asked everyone in the group what veggie they would be. The veggies identified themselves as children of Israel led by Joshua, following God's instruction to go to the Promised Land. The obstacle to the veggies was a fortress called Jericho occupied by the enemy, and weirdly, God's direction was to march around the fortress for six days. The veggies obeyed God's instruction despite not understanding how it would work. As a result, the fortress indeed fell down by itself, and the children of Israel finally came into the Promised Land after 40 years. I was asked first for my thoughts on the video, and even though I did not previously know about the story, I coincidentally had been studying the same underlying truth that day and two days before. I exclaimed loudly to the group that this fairytale was true, and it is still true now, and my confidence about this truth is as much as all the fundamental particles of the whole universe.

All of My Heart

On the first Sunday of 2021, I got $22.24 eBay Bucks that would expire soon. As always, I would use it to purchase some consumer products, but this time, and the first of its kind, I spent it enthusiastically on the ESV Study Bible Hardcover by Crossway. On Monday, the 4th of January, I eagerly messaged Adam via Facebook Messenger to inform him God had answered his prayer for me and that he was a good fisher of men. I stated that God had softened my heart and clearer my eyes to set me free, and if Adam needed some help, I would do what I could. In my heart, I was no longer interested in my job's money-making power nor in pursuing my personal goals. I realized what Adam had been doing over the years despite all life's difficulties was to serve God and His kingdom. Adam replied that he was so encouraged about my message and would like to hear more, so we set up a Facebook video meeting for Wednesday.

I went to the Navigators' website looking for a way to donate some money to Adam, but I could not log in to my account even with a password reset, so I emailed the administrator for help. Previously, I logged in to the account with no problem as I had been donating monthly to 3 different Navigators' staff. I had never donated to Adam, as he never asked or talked about it.

At work, I resumed getting new job assignments, and strangely, when I opened a provided document, it became corrupt, and I could not read the information. I noticed this was a repeat of a mysterious recent occurrence with a previous job assignment. I informed my local office about this and was instructed to ask for the document directly from the client. But even stranger, I was asked via email by a different client of a previously completed assignment to perform additional unusual works on that assignment that I had no idea why. I was informed that these unusual works were requested in the provided original documents, but I could not find them. After emailing back and forth regarding the issue, Carl, the principal engineer in the Chicago office, confirmed that I was never provided that document in the first place. I recalled a long time ago, while I was still working in Las Vegas, Drew, the engineering drafter, had been mysteriously frustrated multiple times despite the fact he was doing his job right and then subsequently was let go from his job. But this time, I knew it was no coincidence. It was the devil bullying a believer when he started to truly see the truth.

Early Wednesday, the 6th of January, I followed the instruction email from the Navigators' website administrator to reset my password to log in to my account, but it did not work. I tried again, but still, nothing changed. As I emailed the administrator again about the problem, I realized the devil was at work against me. He had been deceiving me all my life into not knowing God, committing sins and awaiting death sentence in the end, and now outrageously blocking me from turning to God? How Dare You, Satan! My anger toward the devil exploded like through the whole universe, and I vehemently kneeled down in my living room and exclaimed loudly, "*Father and Lord Jesus, if you are willing, I pledge with all my heart, with all my mind, with all my strength, and with all my soul, to be the Sword of Lord Jesus to take down Satan!*" I was wholeheartedly ready to die in the final battle of my life to avenge the devil no matter what.

Who's The Elect?

My whole self was overwhelmed with this burning determination to fight for God, and as I opened YouTube, this video from Apologia Studios, which I had never known before, called '*Who Are the Elect?*' came up. What was talked about in the video was so new but resonated strangely with me. Wanting to verify where all of this information was from, I reached to my only printed Bible, noticing my initials on the inside of the front and back cover I had written down years ago, opened it, and it was 2 Timothy chapter 2 that titled, '*A Good Soldier of Christ Jesus.*' And as I read it, the author's words became alive as he called me his child and spoke directly to me. The author told me to think over what he said, for the Lord will give me understanding in everything. The author also said he had endured everything for the sake of the elect, and for me personally in this case, that they also may obtain salvation. As I continued to read, I realized the author was the apostle Paul of Jesus Christ, Saint Paul, whom I had always heard and read his name everywhere but did not know who he was until now.

Around 2 PM, Adam messaged me via Facebook, and we video chatted via my desktop computer. Still overwhelmed with the new realization, I told Adam that God had opened my eyes to the truth and set me free. Adam asked what I was set free from, and I answered that I was set free from sins and absolutely confident of my salvation.

In extreme seriousness, I informed Adam the following were bible verses that said about me to the local churches:

"*If we have died with him, we will also live with him; if we endure, we will also reign with him; if we deny him, he also will deny us; if we are faithless, he remains faithful – for he cannot deny himself.*"

I explained that if a local church denied me, I also would deny that church, and if the local church lost faith, I would remain faithful since I could not deny myself. Adam acknowledged me, and I also acknowledged Adam as God's elect and was honored to know him as God had arranged our relationship.

Then, we shared our understanding of what a Good Soldier of Christ Jesus does. Adam explained to me that the soldier is a faithful civil servant who endures all difficulties in his life for the gospel's sake. Adam's understanding of scriptures enlightened me. However, I insisted solemnly that I pledged it all to be the Sword of Lord Jesus Christ to fight the devil in battles and that I was going to a battle soon! Adam responded by praying for me to be a great warrior of God in the spirit world. I had never heard about the spirit world and wondered why Adam never told me about it until now.

Then I expressed my concern to Adam about many innocent people who trust false teachers or attend counterfeit churches, and that they keep donating money while not being saved and not knowing the truth. Feeling deep sorrow for such a tragedy, I cried louder and harder than I ever did in my life. In response, Adam comforted me that these people will be responsible for what they know and what is in their hearts so that they may still be saved. I felt much better, and after some questions regarding Adam's situation, I expressed my intention as a cheerful giver to send Adam money to help with his work. Then, we ended the video chat around 4 PM.

The whole day, I had not been eating anything, not feeling hungry, and only drank water. I did not even think about eating or anything else except my newly found identity and commitment to the heavenly Father and Lord Jesus Christ with my life. Very strangely, I got several alarms on my phone out of nowhere while I surely did not set any alarm, especially never in the middle or late of the day. Recalling my conversation with Adam, I went to the Navigators' website via my desktop computer and called the given number to find a way of sending money to Adam. This was when I felt an increasing presence of evil surrounding me that I never felt before and could not be described by words. While waiting for the answering person on the phone, I also opened my email inbox, and it was unusually flooded with various advertising of consumer products, one of which was from newegg.com. I unsubscribed from these, and they immediately came right back to my inbox. I unsubscribed again, and they came right back again! And again, in my face!

Battling the Devil

Not only did I feel a storm of evil, but they were clearly bullying me live, manifesting in these email responses! Subsequently, a Navigators' operator answered my call, but at that moment, I realized the extreme magnitude and brassiness of evil more than just surrounding myself. In all seriousness and fear, I alerted the Navigators' operator that evil was all out right now, and everyone put on armor, armor for battle, and I needed help! I assumed that the operator was also a believer and would understand my message, but I did not know for sure. I had never felt this fear before, the feeling of powerlessness before a supernatural and evil enemy. What could I do to defend myself in my flesh and bones?

Then I recalled this was exactly what I had asked for! A fight to the death with the devil! I was in fear, but I was also willing to die, and I realized God was the only source of help I could call on. I cried out and prayed, "*Father and Lord Jesus, protect and empower me in this battle. I am ready to die for you!*" Then I stood up on my feet; in my spirit, I saw the great red dragon with seven heads coming at me. With bare hands, I charged and punched through the dragon while cursing him, "*I will kill you, Satan! You will go to the lake of fire!*" I dominated the dragon in the fight, and strangely, I also prayed for him. After a while, I became tired and stopped fighting, and I felt extreme urgency to inform people about this attack from the devil. I had already informed the Navigators' operator and hoped she would spread the message, so I called my colleague. Carl was not answering the phone, so I left a message full of emotion and seriousness. Ron answered the phone, and despite my effort to connect spiritually, he comforted me that business would be taken care of, but I was able to hint that I needed help at the end of the call.

After that, even though I did not see the dragon, I still felt a heavy and dense presence of evil surrounding me. I looked at my phone, and instead of the red rectangular alarm icon, I saw an angrily shaking red bell I had never seen before physically protruding the phone's screen from its surface. I was in fear but also strangely calm, waiting for whatever would come at me at that moment, and then the angry red bell on my phone recessed and disappeared. I understood this as a sign the battle was still on, and it had already become more intense and long enduring. I realized I was calm because I had cast my fear upon God, and then I prayed loudly with vigor and absolute confidence, "*Father and Lord Jesus, in this battle, give me power, strength, speed, endurance, intelligence, weapon, armor, food, water, and everything I need to be victorious!*" I remembered Satan tempted Jesus in the desert and how Jesus defeated him, so I reached for my Bible and found the passage of scriptures I was looking for.

Subsequently, my mind was filled with fear and all kinds of sinful, rebellious, blasphemous thoughts I could imagine. Trying as hard as I could to clear my mind and focus on scriptures, I read aloud, "*Man shall not live by bread alone, but by every word that comes from the mouth of the Father and Lord Jesus Christ.*" Then I repeatedly cried and prayed, "*Father and Lord Jesus, forgive my filthy and blasphemous thoughts, forgive my filthy and blasphemous thoughts.*" Continuing, I read aloud, "*You shall not put the Father and Lord Jesus Christ to the test,*" and read aloud, "*You shall worship the Father and Lord Jesus Christ, and Him only shall you serve.*" Fighting the fear and sinful thoughts in my mind, I repeatedly read these three scripture verses and prayed for forgiveness many times.

After a while, I gradually overcame the fear and sinful thoughts in my mind and became extremely angry with the devil. Once again, in my spirit, I saw the great red dragon with seven heads and I charged at him with all my strength. With bare hands, I tore him into pieces and chopped off his wings and heads multiple times while yelling at him, "*How dare you, Satan! You know who you are messing with!*" Eventually, my anger abated. I no longer felt the presence of evil, and the great red dragon was no more. Left in me only was the deep regret of all the sins and filthy, blasphemous thoughts I had. Continuing non-stop, I cried and prayed for forgiveness. Back to the Bible in my hand and in awe of its potency, I realized its last chapter must be of utmost importance, so I flipped the pages to the book of Revelation. I read the whole book aloud as the Prologue of the book reads: "*Blessed is the one who reads aloud the words of this prophecy, and blessed are those who hear, and who keep what is written in it, for the time is near.*"

The Breath of Life

Around nighttime, I went to the bathroom to shower as usual. However, when I was removing my clothes, my body felt strange and heavier than usual. I looked at my thighs and saw unusual white vapor dissipating on them even though the bathroom was completely dry and I had not touched anything. I saw my thighs were full, firm, round, vibrantly pink in color, and beautiful. Then I looked at my body in the mirror, and my chest was also full, firm, well-defined, vibrantly pink in color, and beautiful. And so were my shoulders and arms. I did not see any dark spots, veins, or blemishes on my body, and I really enjoyed how nice I actually looked. I believed it was the surprising result of my healthy diet and the regular push-ups, sit-ups, and squats I had been doing at home. While taking a shower, I continued crying and praying to Father and Lord Jesus for forgiveness as my mind was still filled with regret about my past. I felt the water from the shower cleanse my body like a baptism, and I thoroughly washed myself.

The next morning, Thursday, the 7th of January, I got a Facebook message from Adam. He sent me a Bible verse related to some of our conversations the previous day. It was Proverbs 11:24 NIV that read, "*One person gives freely, yet gains even more; another withholds unduly, but comes to poverty.*" I took note of this, but the verse did not yet sink into my mind since I had to go on an inspection job shortly after. While traveling and doing inspections on the job, my mind could hardly concentrate; it was filled with reflections and thoughts of what had been happening to me. Once I got home from work, I still did not even think about eating but drank only water. I could not force myself to write the report for the inspection but only read the Bible. I read aloud several times through the book of Revelation, trying hard to understand, took notes with a red pen, and felt better each time.

In the evening, I realized my beautiful body might be the perfected body that I heard about somewhere before. I reasoned that my original body might sustain physical damage or die during the battle with Satan, and the white vapor I saw on my thighs was God's breath that generated the perfected body. I recalled Paul R., who strongly recommended I read through the whole Bible, so I called him to ask questions I wondered about. Paul answered the phone, and I asked about his understanding of the elect. Paul questioned whether I was talking about the government election, and I firmly, clearly answered him: "*Second Timothy, a Good Soldier of Jesus Christ, I AM the elect.*" To which Paul responded, "*Amen!*" Then I told him I was attacked by Satan and asked his understanding about my perfected body. In response, Paul asked if I prayed, and I replied that I prayed for protection and other things. Paul said he knew about people enabled by God to go through walls and other miracles, but not a perfected body as I experienced. Then I asked Paul how to know God's will for me what to do next. Paul was busy and had to go quickly, so he prayed to the heavenly Father to protect me and tell me clearly what to do.

Later, I eagerly went to the bathroom to shower as usual and to examine my perfected body. However, when I removed my clothes, I saw my body was not full, not firm, not well-defined, yellow in color, and having blemishes. I realized it was my original body and a stark contrast with the perfected body I had the night before. I was somewhat disappointed, but the stark contrast mesmerized me even more of what I saw last night, especially by looking at it directly as well as in the mirror.

At night, I could not fall asleep when I went to bed, and I read the Bible verse Adam had sent me in the morning again on my phone. Subsequently, the verse sank in my mind as an instruction from God, and I felt absolutely compelled to obey with all my heart. So, I went to the Navigators website via my desktop computer and found the information to do a wire transfer without the need to log in to my account. My personal checking account at that time had more than $24,000, and I completed the order to transfer this whole amount to Adam, sparing only the changes. I said to myself in my mind that I would still be fine with my regular bi-weekly paychecks coming in. While doing that, I talked aloud to the heavenly Father and Lord Jesus to witness my obedience to the instruction in the Bible verse. Afterward, I sent Adam a Facebook message regarding the transfer and returned to bed. Still thinking about how to communicate with God, I searched the internet via my phone and found an article about God's omnipresence and how a believer can talk to God anytime, anywhere, and then I fell asleep.

The Two Witnesses

The next morning, Friday, the 8th of January, I went on to another inspection job according to schedule. This one was fire damage to a residential dwelling, and while the damage appeared limited in scope from the outside, it was actually severe enough, with toxic chemicals seeping underneath the basement floor, that would warrant a total. There were a number of people at the job site, including the owners and contractors, and via their conversations, I realized there was an insurrection at the Capitol and chaos going on in the federal government. I verbally expressed my disgust and shame for the country of what was happening and, at the end of the inspection, asked everyone for forgiveness of any wrongdoing. On the way out, the owner cried and told me he had gone through multiple troubles with this insurance claim and asked me if I would make a decision as if this was my house, and I nodded. While driving home, I got a call from Tracie, the administrative assistant in the local office, that I was given a break from another scheduled inspection job next week.

Once I got home from work, again, I could not force myself to write any inspection report and only drank water. I reviewed the online article about the attributes of God, which were omnipresence, omniscience, and omnipotence. I realized this was certainly true, and God has been watching all of my actions and thoughts throughout my whole life, and even though not visible to my eyes, both heavenly Father and Lord Jesus were right next to me at the moment. Then I started to have a conversation with them, and instantly, my mind was heightened with answers and understanding. One of my questions was why God did not prevent any evil act or scheme of man, and the answer was that both

Father and Lord Jesus were there witnessing the act for judgment later, but the evil one did not believe in them being there. During the conversation, I also requested that everyone with a good heart will be saved and I will be given a long break from work. After that, I felt tired, so I went to sleep.

In the afternoon that day, I was woken up by Adam's phone call, and we video-chatted via Facebook on my phone. Adam was surprised by the donation I made, but he was caught by even more surprise with my extreme excitement. I informed Adam that the heavenly Father and Lord Jesus were with me at the moment as my two witnesses. And that I had killed the devil in a battle and became victorious, then I was glorified in my perfected body for a day, and everyone with a good heart will be saved. Then I questioned whether Adam believed in God's presence in his everyday life, and Adam answered he had been faithful as if God was present everywhere every day. Adam said he knew that I was the Holy Spirit, which surprised me since I did not know the Holy Spirit was supposed to be a person. I clarified that I was the elect and that the hierarchy of God's elects would be fully revealed later. Adam then said there was a book with popularity only after the Bible about a sinner's journey to knowing God, which sounded like my life. At the end of our conversation, Adam suggested a local church for me to join, which I did not understand why. I felt like there were things Adam knew relevant to me but did not tell me.

The rest of that day and the next day, Saturday, the 9th of January, I continued reading the letters of the apostle Paul in the Bible over and over and took notes with a red pen to understand God's will for me. I understood that God was training me, and I took to heart this verse as God's specific command for me: "*As for you, always be sober-minded, endure suffering, do the work of an evangelist, fulfill your ministry.*" I also called Paul R. again to continue our conversation last time. I was able to fully tell the story that I killed the devil in the battle, which surprised Paul, and I believed this was only one of many battle cycles manifesting eventually to the battle at Armageddon as written in the book of Revelation. I also expressed that true faith will show only through a test staking death or life, and Paul R. agreed. Throughout the day, I still did not want to eat anything but only drink water. I got tired and fell asleep several times.

The Holy Spirit

I woke up at night to go to the bathroom and opened my bedroom door. Strikingly there was a breeze coming through the gap between the door's jamb and panel into my bedroom. There was never any wind like that since this was winter; all windows were closed, and my apartment unit's door and apartment building's doors were all closed. When I got back into the bedroom, I saw the two pull cords of the ceiling fan with light swinging strangely like a pendulum. In physics, a pendulum may swing because of initial energy stipulation, but it would inevitably slow down and then stop, so I watched the two pull cords closely. My bedroom was absolutely quiet with still air, but the longer I watched the pull cords, the more I realized they were swinging supernaturally without any slowing down, just steady back and forth with perfection.

After a long while, I was frightened, realizing the presence of supernatural power in my bedroom. My belief system of reality was shaken to its core, and I lost my grip on what is real in this world, like in a state of insanity. Eventually, I could not tolerate it anymore and grabbed the two pull cords with my hands to stop them. Subsequently, I became mentally grounded, and a flash of an idea came up in my mind that this must have a meaning or something. I pulled the cords and realized I had not turned on the ceiling fan for years since I was very busy working as well as staying overnight in motels. It also made sense to circulate the air due to COVID-19 at the time.

After that, I felt released from the stress, and I was able to sleep for a while, but then I woke up again wanting to read the Bible. I went into the living room and sat down to read. But I felt something unusual interfering with my reading, and I realized my body's left side was being gently tapped. There was nobody around, and the hand tapping me was invisible, but somehow I was not scared. I kept reading, and my body's left side kept being gently tapped, so I realized I must move according to the leading of the tapping. I went back into my bedroom, closed the door, and sat down on my bed along the gap between the bed and the window. Then I moved along the gap to the corner of the bedroom, and my body's left side was no longer being tapped, so I put my feet on the furnace, opened my Bible randomly, and it read '*The Holy District*' in the book of Ezekiel. I had never read most of the Bible and never knew about this book, but I realized it must have a meaning for me, so I kept reading. I interpreted the book as it was giving me instructions on how to allot the land as an inheritance with certain measurements, and I was the Prince with certain religious responsibilities. However, I did not understand why, where, and when were all of these happening.

Subsequently, I got tired and laid down on the bed to rest. Then I felt this infinitely powerful and amazing Spirit that could not be described by words enter and overwhelm my whole mind and body. Then my spirit was like in the cloud and then in the whole universe and beyond. And I felt in complete union with the Spirit of infinite power and possibilities, like I was ascending to God the Father! After a while, I got back to my own mind, and the Spirit made me understand to trust Him only and not to trust even the seriously devoted Christian like Paul R. because my weakness was trusting people.

I got out of bed early the next morning, Sunday, the 10th of January, digesting all that had been happening and wondering who I was. I had a glorified body like being resurrected and then a Spirit of infinite power and possibilities. Am I the second coming Jesus? Trying as hard as I could to clear my mind, I realized I was surely a sinner my whole life, and the thought of being like God was the ultimate blasphemy. I was frightened and waiting for God's judgment to strike me dead right there at that time. But after a while, I was somehow still alive, and I did not know why God's judgment did not come down to me. Then I realized God had mercy and patience for me so that I know He is for me and worthy of my complete surrender and obedience. I recalled the Lord Jesus Christ is the Word of God, integral to who God is, and I took that to my heart.

Urgency of the Gospel

Through my bedroom windows, I saw a very solemn sky and heavy snow going on. I still did not want to eat anything but only drink water. I got back to reading the book of Revelation in the Bible, and this time, I saw a striking similarity between what had happened recently and God's wrath on earth as described in the book. COVID-19 was clearly a pestilence from God, because humans do not possess the ability to create any life form. There was an increase in numbers and sizes of hailstone damage in my inspection job assignments and an increase in numbers and magnitudes of earthquakes all over the world in recent years. I also realized that I had been quarantined in an apartment building with a name literally hinted that I was a Saint, and I reasoned the building was the Holy District assigned to me.

It was clear at that time that the course of my life would not possibly be the same as God had supernaturally interfered with it. I also believed the end time was already here according to the book of Revelation, and I needed to urgently inform the people in the apartment building about it. I felt all human pursuits for money, sex, power, and lies were worthless and disgusting. And I felt deep sorrow for people who did not know the truth. Motivated by this, I brought my Bible with me, walked out of my apartment unit, and started ringing the doorbell of all other apartment units in the building, starting from my floor. Whenever someone opened the door, I extremely solemnly, sometimes crying, informed the person I don't work for money, sex, power, or lie and that the end of the world was coming and the only savior was Jesus Christ, who came down to earth from heaven to die for our sins. Most people either did not open the door or were quickly not interested in what I had to say. During that time, I got really tired and had to come back to rest on my bed several times. I called Paul R. again, telling him what I had been doing, that I had determined to be fully devoted to God and wanted to know what would be typically the next step. Paul supported me in reaching out to all my neighbors and advised me to pray for instructions.

That night, as I continued reading the book of Revelation, this verse really caught my attention: "*("Behold, I am coming like a thief! Blessed is the one who stays awake, keeping his garments on, that he may not go about naked and be seen exposed!").*" I had been recently sleeping naked under my blanket since it was more comfortable than wearing underwear, but this Bible verse told me otherwise. I could not understand why, so I still went to sleep naked but mentally took note of it. Deep in the night, while sleeping with my eyes closed, I somehow saw many transparent dark hands likeness from an invisible pit surrounding my whole body, trying to pull me down. When these hands were about to successfully pull me down, I woke up, realizing my whole pillow was wet with my sweat. I recalled the full-length white as-snow thermal underwear I bought half a year ago, put them on my body, and then went back to sleep. Subsequently, I slept well without any sweating.

Power From on High

The next morning, Monday, the 11th of January, I woke up feeling extremely well and energized. I still had not been eating anything but only drinking water, and I could tell my internal organs had been completely flushed clean. My mind was unusually crystal clear, and my whole body was extremely light and nimble. I recalled, then performed some of my martial arts moves and was amazed at the incredible speed and power I had. Then I visualized some really fancy acrobatic moves that I had only dreamed of being able to do, and amazingly, I did them exactly as visualized. Then I performed some improvised tornado-like moves with my body and arms at incredible speed and power, and my hands started to hurt and turned red like a stovetop. In my spirit, I saw a vast plain and I was on a chariot with full body armor for battle. The enemy was countless coming from afar on the other side. I was ready to instantly charge the enemy, and everything I saw almost became a reality. It was so close at that moment, but it somehow did not happen, and I felt like falling short of something.

After that, by checking my emails, I found that the city of Minneapolis had declared a snow emergency, and the ESV Study Bible Hardcover book I ordered on eBay had arrived in the leasing office. I always parked my Toyota Celica on the street, not driving it, but I needed to prepare to move it during a snow emergency. I put on my jacket and walked out of my apartment building to the street for the first time since all that had happened. Walking outside, I still could feel the unusual clarity of my mind and body with extreme confidence in myself. I reasoned Satan must be out there somewhere, and in my controlled anger, I shouted, "*Satan! Come here! Come here!*" Unexpectedly, the power in my shout was so great it vibrated to the sky and echoed throughout the whole street that I saw someone walking along Homes Park nearby who then glanced around for what was happening.

While removing snow on my Celica, I saw a young man standing across the street next to the Park Meadows Apartments building. I eagerly came to the man to introduce myself as his neighbor and asked if I could pray for him. He peacefully agreed, and I prayed that he would recognize the lies from Satan to know the truth about God. His name was Jeff, and he said he was not a believer in God but just being a good person. Then Jeff offered to help me to move my Celica with full confidence in how effective it would be by pushing it in addition to me driving it out. But puzzling to both of us, even though Jeff pushed it so hard that his whole face turned red, the car only moved back and forth in its same place. Jeff eventually gave up, and I could not drive my Celica out of its place either. After that, I tried to pray for a few other people I saw around but was rejected.

Later, I walked into the leasing office to get my ESV Study Bible Hardcover book. There, I met Kelly, the owner and manager. I eagerly asked if I could pray for her, and she peacefully agreed. I prayed that she would recognize the lies from Satan to know the truth about God. During our short conversation, Kelly said she was Catholic and the difference between Catholic and Christianity I knew was that Catholics pray to Mother Mary. Subsequently, I returned to my apartment building and continued to ring doorbells on the units that previously had nobody home. After all my preaching and praying efforts over two days, there was John, who lived next to my apartment unit listened to me, but he said he was fine and did not need prayer. There were EJ on the basement level and Niko on the top floor, who listened and accepted my prayer that they would see the lies from Satan to know the truth about God.

The Decision

That night, while lying on my bed to sleep, I reached for my original Bible and was determined to read the whole book aloud. I had finished reading the book of Revelation several times, so I turned over to the front to read the book of Genesis. I read aloud: "*In the beginning, God created the heavens and the earth...*" Then I cried deeply for what was the simple but profound truth that the human race trampled on as hard as they could over the course of history up to the present. Deep in the night, I could not sleep and felt the urge to commit my life to save my neighbor from Satan. So, I got out of bed and printed a large black text on a standard-size white paper: "*This is Tony, your neighbor. You are welcome in here anytime.*" Then I put this label on the front of my apartment unit's door and taped it on with clear tape. Subsequently, I was able to continue sleeping that night.

The next morning, Tuesday the 12th of January, I was woken up by a phone call. It was my company's client from an insurance carrier asking about an inspection job. I told the client that I no longer worked for money, sex, power, or lies and I would go to save my neighbor and study the Bible full-time. The client said, "*Good luck with that,*" and then hung up. After that, I got a call from Tracie, the local office's administrative assistant, about the matter, and I told her the most important things are: God and our neighbor. Tracie said I needed to provide notice one month in advance, but I refused. Subsequently, Ron, my boss, called me, and I confirmed that I just made my decision last night. Ron seemed to understand the deeper reason behind my decision and then proceeded to inform the company's Human Resources.

Several hours later, I heard my apartment unit's doorbell ring. I opened the door, and there was Steve, the fire team leader in my company's local office. I invited Steve to come in, but he did not do so. It was clear that Steve came to take away all of the company's properties given to me, including a laptop, cell phone, camera, shoes, ladders, equipment, and protective clothing for my job. I solemnly gathered and gave everything to Steve. At this point, Steve seemed to realize the seriousness and deeper reason behind my decision. When we got outside to the parking lot to transfer equipment from my Toyota 4Runner to the company's truck, I saw compassion from Steve, so I asked to pray for him and he agreed. I prayed that Steve would recognize the supernatural influence of Satan on him so that God may save him then I cried aloud. My crying was interrupted gently by Steve, and then he drove away.

Back to my apartment unit, I continued reading the book of Genesis aloud until I felt satisfied. Then I closed my bedroom door, went to the corner of my bed, put my feet on the furnace, and prayed to the heavenly Father and Lord Jesus. I took note of what I had prayed and added more prayers I wanted to pray next time. Then I had some messages via Facebook with Adam arranging a meeting time in my apartment, and I informed him I quit my job to serve God only. Later in the day, I realized I had lost a lot of weight after not eating anything for almost a week. So, I went out to get some organic bread to eat. It was the best-tasting bread or food I ever had in my life, and I quickly finished the whole loaf. While driving outside, I saw some miserable people standing on street corners asking for help, so I purchased more of the same loaves of bread to give them. Whenever I gave out the bread, I felt full of compassion and emotionally moved like never before.

The next day, I continued reading my original Bible aloud and prayed behind closed doors with my feet on the furnace at the corner of my bedroom. I made these two activities my daily routine, and I resumed eating a lot of organic hard-boiled eggs regularly, like before, to regain my weight. After adding my Celica to the insurance policy with my 4Runner, I was able to move the car out of its place. I also recovered my 8-year-old cellphone, a Nokia 920, and my old phone number from Google Voice to use with a prepaid cell phone service. Unexpectedly, I got an email from Kelly, the owner and manager of my apartment complex, warning that she got feedback from some of my neighbors and

I should refrain from soliciting anything. That evening during the Navigators' Zoom meeting, '*Trusting in God,*' I emotionally shared with the group how I quit my job and was enlisted in God's army.

Anxious About Tomorrow

Later that week, I realized that by quitting my job after donating all my money, I had put myself in a difficult situation, so I panicked. In my mind, I questioned why I did that and how I could continue to live as I still had rent, food, utilities, and other monthly expenses. I had the urge to just go back to the way it was to find financial security in a job. Subsequently, Adam visited me in my apartment for the first time, so we talked, and I shared with him some of what had happened to me, including my panic. Adam pointed me to these Bible verses, and they read: "*But seek first the kingdom of God and his righteousness, and all these things will be added to you. Therefore, do not be anxious about tomorrow, for tomorrow will be anxious for itself. Sufficient for the day is its own trouble.*"

So, after Adam had left, I memorized these verses and uttered them aloud repeatedly to fight against my panic. By mealtime, I started to crack and peel my hard-boiled eggs for preparation. As usual, there were always some full round eggs and some slim oblong eggs, which I always cracked last. While peeling the eggs, I was still panicking and saying these Bible verses aloud. Then I gradually noticed the peeled eggs seemed to become fuller and rounder than before they were cracked, so I took mental note of the most oblong and slim egg I left for the last. When I cracked this last egg and peeled it, the egg indeed became perfectly full and round in my hand, just like the other full round eggs, and I cried. After that, I felt much better and was no longer panicking.

A couple of weeks later, I got my last paycheck from EFI Global, including a payout for all my paid time off, totaling more than $6000. I disassembled my newly built personal computer and sold off its components to get some more money. I also still had financial assets in my retirement and health saving account, which I could withdraw at a penalty tax to live off for the near future. Sometimes there were still sinful or rebellious thoughts that came up in my mind. Knowing these were not from God, I said aloud: "*Get out, Satan! You go to the lake of fire! Heavenly Father and Lord Jesus are here with me!*" And it worked every time, driving away these thoughts. Around this time, The U of M Navigators resumed weekly meetings in person, and I was able to share some of what happened to people. Besides Adam, among Navigators staff, there was Trevor L., who listened to my long story and commented that I seek God. I also visited Paul R. a few times at his Risen Church's office to talk and learn from his experience.

A New Beginning

On February 5, 2021, out of the blue, I recalled Heather, whom I first met six years before, and was so impressed with her serving of traditional Vietnamese food that led to local communities of believers and all that happened to me. The last time we saw each other was in 2017 during the Cru retreat, so I sent her a message via Facebook that I had recently joined the army of the Lord and I only serve the heavenly Father and Lord Jesus Christ. Unexpectedly, Heather replied that she was just talking about me and that she had some friends who just moved to Minneapolis to learn Vietnamese, specifically the Northern Dialect, before moving to Vietnam. Subsequently, Heather provided me with the contact information of her friends, Alex and Brittany, so we could connect and arrange language lessons.

Near the end of the month, I met Alex and Brittany and their three small children, and we immediately built a great connection and shared mutual faith. From then on, I visited their place regularly three times a week in the afternoon to help them learn basic Vietnamese vocabulary, grammar, speaking, and writing according to a chosen curriculum. Alex and Brittany told me that Heather and her friends' group had already moved to Thai Nguyen, Vietnam, for a while and were adapting to living there. Coincidentally, my father had a vacation home in Thai Nguyen and went there occasionally, so I subsequently connected my father and Heather via Facebook. Around this time, I received an email and a letter from two Navigators missionaries abroad thanking me for financial support indirectly via Adam. Adam let me know my donation would be used where there were needs, including continued support for the English Club.

Also, in early February 2021, I had the urge to tell all that happened to as many people as possible. I knew this was of utmost significance as it testified to the literal truth and interpretation of the Bible. I never had the thought of a miracle occurring in modern times, much less occurring to me that I had seen with my own eyes and felt with my own flesh. I understood a believer has a responsibility to testify the truth about God, and I thought about writing a memo of all the miracles I witnessed. So, along with my daily prayers, I also prayed for instructions and guidance on how to testify according to God's will.

On February 16, 2021, at 2:15 PM, while shopping for groceries at Costco, out of the blue, I received a text message on my cell phone:

"Hi Tony, You have a book in your head, we can get it on paper. Hire a top professional writer for your book. Activate now: https://pzary.com."

When I read the text message, I was filled with peace and joy, realizing this was no coincidence. The message was delivered on my old phone and an old number that I had not used for years, and I never had any text advertisement like this before. However, I was a little surprised that the text message suggested a book rather than just a memo.

The Book Writing Process

When I got home, I followed the website link in the text message and was redirected to the website of Iconic Ghostwriter Company, where I was offered a book writing and publishing package at a special discount for $1,850 including free 300 prints of the book. After talking with a representative and some screening of the company's credibility, I took the offer and paid for the contract but the written contract shown on the website itself was never sent to me. There was some back and forth between me and the company regarding how the book would be written in the following months. After reading the half-done chapter 1 written by the company, I realized that what I want to present in the book can only be written by myself, and I proceeded to do so. Later, when I requested the original contract, I was sent a different contract in the name of Professional Ghost Writer testifying for my original payment and date but without the free 300 prints. Everything looked very similar and I was focusing hard on writing the book so I did not pay close attention to it.

In May 2022 and in July 2022 I was asked to make an additional $500 payment for ISBN codes and $300 payment for unlimited cover art editing respectively, even though the contract said unlimited revisions, creative cover design, publishing on Amazon, Kindle, Barnes and Noble & Google books, etc. I made payments as requested because I did not recall the contract at the time and wanted the book to be published soon. By August 2022, I completed the draft writing of the book with 12 chapters and sent it to the company. Later I also was asked to pay $2,500 per year for online marketing of the book but I declined. A whole year long after that was the slow process of editing my initial draft where I ended up doing almost all the work and more. Because the editor assigned to me either did not bother or was incapable of doing decent work or both. Relevant details in my writing were deleted, poor or wrong interpretations were added with even incorrect grammar and spelling! I was very patient and went along to correct all of these as I thought the unique nature of my book would not be easy to fully comprehend at first.

The very slow editing process had unexpected benefits that I was able to include my two letters to the local churches later as well as make my original draft be more complete. I did get help from the company with some basic written English and the book's cover art was done well according to my design concept. But even when the book got into the formatting stage, where the professional ghostwriters supposed to fully take care of business, the same pattern of unprofessional work was presented: mismatch chapter numbers in the page header, mismatch and misaligned footer numbers, missing spaces between sub-chapters, etc. I decided to find online reviews of the company's works and found on the website of trustpilot.com many negative reviews that described exactly my bad experiences with them.

As of this writing near the end of September 2023, when I strongly pointed out their bad works and disregard for my instructions, they actually presented these as if they were my fault. That was when I fully confirmed they knew exactly what they were doing the whole time. I also recall now that they promised 100% profit of book sales to the author on their original website advertisement and via phone conversation but this term is not shown on the actual written contract that they sent me later. It would be a big mistake to trust them to give me full copyrights or any right according to their promises if they were the one who owns all online accounts when publishing the book. So, I decided to go through the publication process myself just like other adverse processes I went through in the past that made me the person I am today.

Afterword

Since the actual time of miracles described in the last chapter of this book to this writing as of August 2022, I have experienced some other miraculous incidents. I want to describe two of them here, along with my interpretation of their significance and self-interpretation of my life story.

Easter Observance

In April 2021, when I knew about Easter coming soon as a yearly Christian festival commemorating the resurrection of Jesus from the dead, I decided to fast intentionally for the first time in my life. I thought it would be quite easy as I previously fasted for almost a week, even though not intentionally, as described in the last chapter. So, I started not eating anything from Friday, April 2nd, and only drank water. By Saturday, the next day, I felt hunger and discomfort in my entire body, and by the end of the day, I felt like being sick. I originally planned to fast for three days until Monday, but by midday Sunday, April 4th, I could not tolerate the hunger and discomfort anymore, so I ate and broke the fast there.

After breaking the fast, and when I finished eating, I found two big swollen areas like bubbles on my neck right under my jaw that shocked and scared me. I never had anything like that before and could not comprehend why and how it could happen so fast. I did some quick search on the internet about the phenomenon and found out it may indicate I had a serious illness or cancer. The bubbles increasingly hurt my neck, and I felt extremely uncomfortable; I was really worried and looking for help. I thought about going to a doctor, but that seemed to be taking too long for this urgent problem, so I thought that God would certainly know what was going on and would help me if that was consistent with his will. So, I prayed earnestly to the heavenly Father and Lord Jesus Christ to heal my neck rather than letting me die from this illness. After I prayed, the bubbles on my neck went away just as quickly as when they came, and I felt so relieved from the trouble.

After that incident, I wondered why I seemingly got punished for sincerely worshiping God by fasting, and at the same time, God had the mercy to heal me of my affliction. Through my continuous reading of the Bible and investigating the origin of Christian holidays, I discovered that Easter has pagan roots. Contemporary traditions such as the Easter Bunny and the Easter egg can also be traced back to the practices established by Semiramis. Because of their prolific nature, rabbits have long been associated with fertility and its goddess Ishtar (Easter), and the people worshiped Semiramis as the goddess of fertility. Scripture in John 4:24 reads: "*God is spirit, and those who worship him must worship in spirit* ***and*** *truth.*" So, although I worshiped God in spirit during Easter 2021, I did not worship God in truth because Easter's origin had nothing to do with the Lord Jesus Christ but with a pagan female god.

Some Christians argue that what matters for the Christian holidays, even though they may have pagan roots, is that celebrating Jesus is all you think about. This is clearly wrong according to the scriptures, and I will illustrate this: Believers, the church, is called the bride of Christ to represent this exclusive and intimate relationship. So, let's say you have a beautiful wife, and even though she loves you in her heart, due to her ignorance or complacency, she sleeps with someone else, thinking it's you or acceptable as you as long as all she thinks about is you. Not only does she do it as a habit, but she also gives you hugs and kisses on the cheek while continuing to get physically intimate with someone else.

Crypto Boom

In June 2021, I realized there was a huge ongoing boom in crypto-currency prices as well as a scarcity and extremely inflated prices of graphics cards. More and more people had spent a lot of money buying as many modern graphics cards as possible at double to triple the list price to build crypto mining rigs and make great profits. Doing some searches online, I found that I could pre-order some newly released professional graphics cards at provantage.com at the list price to build a crypto mining rig and make an income stream out of it. So, I went ahead and used my credit card to make an order of around $9,000. However, I still need to purchase other necessary hardware to build the rig and then learn how to operate and maintain it.

The following days after putting in that order, my mind became unsettled. My rationalization of building the crypto mining rig to make money as I was no longer working seemed legitimate, but I still felt something was not right about that. When I questioned myself whether doing this would please the heavenly Father, my honest answer was that it would take much of my time and attention while I needed to concentrate on doing the two jobs that God had given me, which are writing this book and teaching Vietnamese to Alex and Brittany. Subsequently, I was convinced I must repent from this idolatry and excuse. That night, I went to the corner of my bedroom and prayed decisively that God would give me the power to resist this temptation and that He would thwart what I had planned to do.

The next morning, I woke up feeling resolute, and immediately, the first thing I did was calling provantage.com to cancel my order. After canceling the order and my plan of building a crypto-mining rig, I felt much relief from guilt. That night, lying in bed to sleep, I stretched out my legs like doing a side split to relax, just as I sometimes did years ago while practicing Taekwondo to improve my flexibility. When I woke up the next morning, I felt a strange, pleasant feeling in my right hip joint. When I looked at my underwear area along my right hip joint, I saw moisture like sweat, but it was completely dry on the left hip joint and anywhere else. So I went to the living room, sat on my sofa, and stretched out my legs like doing a side split. Wonderfully, my right hip joint popped in a sound and opened up well past its previous limit, which was incurred from my back injury in 2014.

After that, I wondered about the explanation and meaning of the healing. The moisture on my right hip joint was like the white vapor on my thighs when I saw my glorified body. I never had anything peculiar like that before and could not imagine how to recreate the same effect, so it was God's breath. But God could have healed me without His breath like He previously healed my neck, so this was a visible sign of blessing and encouragement after I had successfully resisted temptation. Also, my extended interpretation of this matter is that humans have increasingly put more value and importance on the digital world they created, which is dead and infinitely inferior compared to God's creation of life and the physical world that makes the digital world possible. This is the next level form of human rebellion against God.

The Whole Story

So, what would be the interpretation of my whole life story, including all the miraculous occurrences and beyond? That is a great question that I still have been un-puzzling up until the present. I recall here a number of biblical and spiritual coincidences that can be derived from my life story to shed light on the matter.

From my date of birth November 25, 1980 in Vietnam to January 4, 2021 in the U.S., when I wholeheartedly turned to God and was set free from the power of sin, it was the onset of 40 years and 40 days. Note that Vietnam time is around 12 hours ahead of U.S. time. And the devil was the last fortress blocking anyone from entering God's kingdom. Only after spiritually defeating the devil on January 6, 2021, when I saw God's breath and my glorified body, that I had officially entered. As described in the Bible, it took God's chosen people, the Israelites, 40 years in the wilderness before they got into the land promised by God. Satan tempted Jesus in the wilderness for 40 days. There are also many other occurrences of 40 years as well as 40 days in the Bible.

Why did I end up traveling halfway around the earth to live and meet God? Recalling the U.S. involvement in the Vietnam War and the bombing of Hanoi, where I was born, which was ordered by Richard Nixon. It was the largest heavy bomber strike that the U.S. Air Force launched since World War II. These B-52 Stratofortress bombers were literal metal dragons of mass destruction that destroyed many homes and killed thousands of innocent Vietnamese civilians, including women and children. If the U.S. had succeeded in the war and the bombing of Hanoi continued longer, I likely could not have been born. Scripture in Revelation 12:17 reads, "*Then the dragon became furious with the woman and went off to make war on the rest of her offspring, on those who keep the commandments of God and hold to the testimony of Jesus.*"

So God raised me up into this world from the poverty and ruin of Hanoi after the war. This likely explained why I felt like waiting in darkness and nothingness for an eternity before birth. And with perfect timing, God showed whom He has chosen to the American, including those who know the truth of the gospel, claiming to be Christians yet do the devil's will. Scripture in 1 Corinthians 1:27 reads, "*But God chose what is foolish in the world to shame the wise; God chose what is weak in the world to shame the strong.*"

God promised not to forget me as the only child of a troubling marriage and a neglectful mother. Scripture in Isaiah 49:15 reads, "*Can a woman forget her nursing child, that she should have no compassion on the son of her womb? Even these may forget, yet I will not forget you.*" Growing up not knowing God, I inevitably sinned and was baited by the devil's filth and the false promise of worldly success. Ironically, through this process, I was strengthened in spirit and came to the U.S. to experience the inner workings of the devil as well as the truth of God.

Seemingly like a coincidence throughout my life, earthquakes have been brought to my attention in one way or another, from my unlikely childhood experience to my specialized study in graduate school. This is how God has always warned me of His power and righteous anger to come. Scripture in Revelation 16:18 reads, "*And there were flashes of lightning, rumblings, peals of thunder, and a great earthquake such as there had never been since man was on the earth, so great was that earthquake.*"

Also, I did many hail damage inspections during my last engineering job. Scripture in Revelation 16:21 reads, "*And great hailstones, about one hundred pounds each, fell from heaven on people; and they cursed God for the plague of hail because the plague was so severe.*"

My spiritual identity started forming even before being exposed to Christianity. When I obtained U.S. citizenship in 2013, I also officially changed my name during the naturalization process to Tony, a common short for Anthony. It is at the Saint Anthony Village Apartments, where I am still living right now, that I met God, the invisible person Holy Spirit, and experienced miracles. My online avatar portraying a white lion's head, which I started using in 2014, is consistent with the symbol of the Israelite tribe of Judah. In 2015, I founded the Vanduul Conquerors organization to fight against the powerful and evil alien Vanduul in the Star Citizen game universe. Scripture in Revelation 21:7 reads, "*The one who conquers will have this heritage, and I will be his God, and he will be my son.*"

What astonished me to this day was how speedily God answered my wholehearted prayer to be the Sword of Lord Jesus Christ to take down Satan. I expected a battle with the devil to start in the near unknown future from the time of my prayer, but God gave it the same day, January 6, 2021. I also perceive this was a test of my faith in God that I subsequently passed. This will not be the last of my fight with the devil, but surely, there are more to come until the end. Scripture in Revelation 2:26 reads, "*The one who conquers and who keeps my works until the end, to him I will give authority over the nations.*"

Also astonishing to me is how my experience with the Holy Spirit was exactly as foretold by what Jesus said in John 14:20-21 "*In that day you will know that I am in my Father, and you in me, and I in you. Whoever has my commandments and keeps them, he it is who loves me. And he who loves me will be loved by my Father, and I will love him and manifest myself to him.*"

Seemingly, my life was predestined to fulfill certain scriptures, but I want to stress that God's sovereignty and foreknowledge do not contradict or excuse human's responsibility for life choices. I did not choose from which parents, where, and what time I was born. But I did choose and was responsible for all of my actions, words, and thoughts, as these are abilities granted by God and are independent of life circumstances. Just as God granted Adam and Eve the choice to obey God or the devil, and once they ate the forbidden fruit to have knowledge of good and evil, they were responsible for their evil choices. God has been calling me throughout my life, but He only supernaturally revealed Himself to me **after** I had genuinely repented and entrusted my life to Him.

In Closing

Now, regarding all the people I mentioned in this book, some may seem more favorable and others less so. By no means did what I had written about someone in this book define who they were or fully describe them at the time. However, I truthfully wrote down what I saw, heard, felt, and thought according to the time, view angle, and situation that occurred to me. Jesus said in Matthew 10:26-28, "*So have no fear of them, for nothing is covered that will not be revealed, or hidden that will not be known. What I tell you in the dark, say in the light, and what you hear whispered, proclaim on the housetops. And do not fear those who kill the body but cannot kill the soul. Rather fear Him who can destroy both soul and body in hell.*"

All people have sinned and fallen short of the glory of God, and whoever truly believes to be the few saved from the coming wrath of God shall change from their sinful and rebellious ways to wholeheartedly live out the teachings of the Lord Jesus Christ. There is much I want to talk about theology, correct understanding, and application of scriptures, particularly in the American religious scene today, but these are outside the intended scope of this book as an eyewitness account. This is just the start of my ministry, so more work I shall do until the end.

Update to this book as of June 2023, I included after this as extra content my first and second letter to the local churches, which I completed in January and June of 2023, respectively.

First Letter to the Local Churches

I am writing this letter to local believers in America who still have the love of God in their hearts. By the mercy and grace of God, I, who was once lost for decades, now have been found and being saved by Him.

I also benefited greatly from various communities of believers and information sources in America, which challenged my existing beliefs and opened my eyes to things beyond my imagination. If I had not had such exposure, I would still live in ignorance and deadly sins on my way to eternal damnation.

It is not a coincidence that I was grafted into the body of American believers while having a foreign upbringing and experience. Thanks to God for opening my eyes, I have come to realize various errors in the commonly held doctrines and practices of American believers that I know of.

Understand that the spirit of errors originated from the devil, who is far more crafty and powerful than any human. The devil knows the truth and uses scriptures with false reasoning to deceive believers. Also, the human flesh strongly resists being crucified and wants to believe the lies from the devil instead.

For those who did not know, Jesus is not the true name of the Messiah but a transliteration created several hundred years ago, which materially changed the original name's pronunciation. The Savior's name is Yehoshua (Yeh-HO-shoo-ah), and its short form is Yeshua (Yeh-SHOO-ah).

Now, within the scope of this letter and not always citing the corresponding scriptures, it is my turn to present here some major issues with patience and love for those who would receive me.

God Does Not Change

Yeshua said in John 8:58, "*Truly, truly, I say to you, before Abraham was, I am,*" and in John 10:30, "*I and the Father are one.*" Where was Yeshua during the entire time of the Old Testament, and when God gave commandments to the Israelites? Answer: Yeshua was all and every word that came from the mouth of God to create the world and communicate with the Israelite people. John 1:3 says, "*All things were made through him, and without him was not anything made that was made.*"

God does not change, including His Law and commandments given to believers in the Old Testament. Numbers 23:19 says, "*God is not man, that he should lie, or a son of man, that he should change his mind. Has he said, and will he not do it? Or has he spoken, and will he not fulfill it?*"

Yeshua did not come to abolish the Old Testament Laws but to fulfill them. These Laws stand until the current heavens and earth pass away. Yeshua said in Matthew 5:17, "*Do not think that I have come to abolish the Law or the Prophets; I have not come to abolish them but to fulfill them.*" You can investigate the meaning of the original Greek or Hebrew word that was translated as fulfill, but roughly, it means: to enforce.

How does Yeshua enforce the Old Testament Laws? Answer: First, by living out His life as an example for believers to follow. Second, by writing the laws and statutes on their hearts. Third, by dying on the cross as atonement for sins. Fourth, by coming back again to execute judgment on those who knowingly or not still practice sin. When Yeshua comes back in the near future, His atonement for sins comes to an end.

Grace and Repentance

This grace of forgiveness God offered to us, because all have sinned and God so loved the world, has two clauses. The first clause is the grace period; it ends when a person dies or when Yeshua returns. The second clause is repentance; those who receive forgiveness must successfully repent of all deadly sins as a minimum so that God's law is enforced. **Repent or perish is the essence of the gospel of Christ**.

Understand that sin is **any** transgression of God's law, commandment, or instruction. Committing a sin in ignorance is still a sin, and willfully or repeatedly committing a sin makes it a more serious one. There are sins that are not deadly, and there are God's instructions that mean only for certain situations.

An argument against what was presented previously is that salvation is through faith alone, not because of works. Answer: yes, and the deception is false reasoning regarding faith and works. Salvation to eternal life requires the supernatural work of God. The world's super-rich could literally do any work a billion times more than the poor so they can have eternal life, can't they? Human work cannot save.

To be clear, there are two types of work here. Works that are in accordance with the commandments of God and works that are in accordance with the traditions or commandments of men, like that of the scribes and Pharisees. The former is evidence of faith in God; the latter is evidence of faith in men. Biblical faith is not just believing the truth but also manifests in doing what the Word of God had commanded.

On the Day of Judgment, Yeshua tells many professing Christians to depart. The reason is clear: continuing violation of the Law. Yeshua said in Matthew 7:23, "*I never knew you; depart from me, you* ***workers of lawlessness***." Even though these people did many works in Yeshua's name, they still live in deadly transgression of at least one of God's laws, commandments, or instructions. This is consistent with what Yeshua said in Luke 13:24, "*Strive to enter through the narrow door. For many, I tell you, will seek to enter and will not be able.*"

One could object to the above; how all of my good work and obedience do not count if I have just one sin remaining? Think about this in America: You perfectly obeyed all the laws, paid all due taxes, and volunteered in public services. However, once in your life, you committed just one deadly crime, but you never do it again, and the crime is discovered years later. Shall you be set free from your crime?

How good is the news that God let someone die in your place so that your crime is forgiven, with one condition that you shall never commit any crime anymore? Is that even allowed in American laws? Now think about true Christians in other regions of the world who are being persecuted daily. Yet many American Christians say they shall be allowed to practice at least one sin of their preference and still enter "Heaven."

Who's The Judge?

Furthermore, secular people believe they won't go to "Hell" because they generally live a good moral life. And professing Christians have no doubt they are going to "Heaven" as they have no deadly sin. Is that so? Who is the judge of what is sin and what is deadly? Is that the Word of God or the self-definition of men? Most Christians disbelieve there are deadly sins they are living in, and that's exactly why it is so.

Understand there is a deadly difference between the law of this world and the Law of God. Being considered good and moral by this world and its religious organizations contributes to a false perception of being in the right standing with God. Yeshua said to the religious professionals of His day in Luke 16:15, "*You are those who justify yourselves before men, but God knows your hearts. For what is exalted among men is an abomination in the sight of God.*"

The point is this: it is bad, not good, for Christians to comfort each other that we have security in salvation just because we are sincere in our belief. Will professing Christians submit to the truth revealed in God's words that the vast majority of them will not be saved? Yeshua said in Matthew 7:14, "*For the gate is narrow, and the way is hard that leads to life, and those who find it are few.*"

What really matters are the truth and obedience to the truth. Sincere faith and works in errors or deceptions surely will not save. Rather, we need to let God's law and commandments judge us, to surely find out sins in our blind spots, and then take corrective actions. That's how we have true security by the work in progress of our sanctification rather than stagnation. Paul said in 2 Corinthians 13:5, "*Examine yourselves, to see whether you are in the faith. Test yourselves.*"

Sins in Blind Spots

So, what are the sins in our blind spots? Answer: they vary according to each congregation and the individual believer. The devil is the god of this world, and his agents have been all out lying to everyone. Our current sins vary according to what lies from the devil we still believe in. The serpent has been doing the same trick since the Garden of Eden. And even though God's instructions were crystal clear in His words, we sin when our unwillingness to obey accepts the rationalization presented by the serpent and acts on it.

Most unbelievers would agree that murdering, stealing, or lying are wrong. And most Christians would agree with 9 of the 10 Commandments of God, except the 4th commandment to keep the Sabbath day holy. What is common between the two groups' standards of right and wrong? Answer: it's their own standard. Remember, whoever, knowingly or not, fails to repent of just one deadly sin will not be saved.

All I presented previously are sufficient to show why violating God's 4th or any commandment is a sin. However, I also want to rebuke the root of the popular Christian argument that Yeshua is Lord of the Sabbath, so He did away with it; Or it's a ceremonial law that Yeshua already fulfilled; Or Yeshua Himself is the Sabbath rest for Christians, so it is no more.

Lawful Sabbath

What did Yeshua do and say on the Sabbath as described in the scriptures? He healed the sick and the demon-oppressed. He said, "*It is lawful to do good on the Sabbath*" and "*The Sabbath was made for man, not man for the Sabbath.*" He told stories in the Old Testament about how exceptions to the appearance of the Law were made in cases of emergency. He pointed out that those who accused him would do the same for their sheep.

The "do good" that Yeshua said serves the legitimate needs of other people in dire situations without expecting anything in return. In contrast to men, they often "do good" by crediting themselves for providing products or services to worldly desires or practices, and to make the most profits. Even religious works to support oneself and family or charity works for recognition are not recognized as good by God.

In a business culture like that of corporate America, it is not too uncommon that someone dies from overworking. So men were sacrificed for money. It is clear how a full day of rest may save lives, and the commandment to rest from usual work is a moral law. The scribes and Pharisees, however, used this as an excuse. While they "do good" for their livestock, they would rather sacrifice people with urgent needs on the Sabbath for the sake of their traditions and systems of power.

Christian Holidays

For those who did not know, you shall investigate the origin of all "Christian" holidays. They are well-documented and historically verifiable. Scriptures clearly indicate our Savior was not born during the winter. The churches in the New Testament and early churches in America never celebrated Christmas and the like. In fact, celebrating Christmas was made illegal by conservative Christians in the past.

Jeremiah 10:2-3 tells, "*Thus says the Lord: Learn not the way of the nations ... for the customs of the peoples are vanity...*" Yeshua said in John 4:24, "*God is spirit, and those who worship him must worship in spirit and truth,*" and in John 14:17, "*Even the Spirit of truth, whom the world cannot receive...*" Again, what really matters is obedience to the truth. However, there is no truth in the world and its customs.

Knowledgeable Christians all admit "Christian" holidays have pagan roots. However, despite the above words of God, the majority of them still practice the traditions to some extent. Their primary supporting argument is to adapt to the culture for the sake of the gospel. What gospel is being conveyed here?

Yeshua said in Matthew 5:13, "*You are the salt of the earth, but if salt has lost its taste, how shall its saltiness be restored?...*" Paul said in 2 Corinthians 6:14, "*Do not be unequally yoked with unbelievers...*" and during his ministries to the Gentiles, he told them to their faces that their religious practices were wrong.

So, followers of Yeshua are called to be salty and live holy, different from that of the world. We live in the world and evangelize the world so that unbelievers would change how they live, not the other way around. By living like the world while claiming to be saved, Christians are conveying a different gospel.

Work Out Your Salvation

Just several years ago, I was new to Christianity and practiced all the popular things in the world. By the grace and mercy of God, I am realizing more of my sins and making changes accordingly. These changes cost me financially and socially, but they are nothing in comparison to security in God's hands. My blessings come from desiring God's ways, which are truly good for me, and despising men's ways, which are destructions coated in temporary worldly benefits.

I highly praise American Christians who are still faithful in their evangelism, hospitality, and correct teaching of scriptures. These are difficult works showing obedience to God's commandments. So, if any error is recognized by these believers, I have faith that they would be willing to and step-by-step make the changes to correct it.

I could not stress enough that we humans, by nature, are children of wrath. We are a sinful and right-in-our-own-eyes bunch. Isaiah 55:8 tells, "*For my thoughts are not your thoughts, neither are your ways my ways, declares the Lord.*" We indeed need to deny ourselves and take up our cross daily in order to obey God's commandments. Our natural inclinations are disbelief and disobedience toward God's words.

Finally, understand that I am not the judge; God is. I am working out my own salvation with fear and trembling. And final judgment is not yet until Yeshua returns. However, scriptures are clear and sufficient for a believer to make a judgment regarding what is false and what is true. Given the information, one can tell whether someone is currently on the narrow and hard road that leads to life or the broad road that leads to destruction.

Second Letter to the Local Churches

This is a follow-up to my first letter to local believers in America who still have the love of God in their hearts. It is my response to the feedback I received and to extend beyond the previous letter's scope.

For those who did not know, in Exodus 3:15, God the Father did disclose His name and told Moses to tell the children of Israel for remembrance to all generations. His name had been mostly replaced with terms like YHWH omitting the vowels, or LORD, or Adonai by the scribes and translators over many generations. According to the Hebrew sources I found, the Father's name is Yehovah.

There Is Nothing New

I was asked the question, so what's new? The Answer is in Ecclesiastes 1:9, "*What has been is what will be, and what has been done is what will be done, and there is nothing new under the sun.*" God the Almighty, the beginning and the end, knows and controls all before He created the world. In the same way, how mankind sinned and how one can be saved stay the same, from Adam to the last person on earth.

Adam and Eve used to live in a close relationship with God. They lived out the human abilities God had given them, to be fruitful, multiply, and have dominion over the earth according to God's original commandment. God also gave them another commandment not to eat the forbidden fruit, and death is the consequence of disobeying. God gave them the commandments through His spoken words.

Adam and Eve kept God's commandments until they listened to the serpent. The serpent told them some truths mixed with one lie that they would not die by disobeying God's commandment. The lie is a direct contradiction to God's previously spoken words. Subsequently, they believed the serpent and disbelieved God's words. Their new faith in the serpent manifested in them eating the forbidden fruit.

This was what the serpent said in Genesis 3:4-5, "*You will not surely die. For God knows that when you eat of it, your eyes will be opened, and you will be like God, knowing good and evil.*" This is scripture and biblical; does that mean these are God's words? Answer: No, these are the words that came from the mouth of the enemy. Scriptures record what happened, including God's words and many other things.

By doing to the contrary of God's commandment while having the ability not to, Adam and Eve had essentially tested God to see if His words were true or compromised. It showed that they did not fear God. Ecclesiastes 12:13 says, "*The end of the matter; all has been heard. Fear God and keep his commandments, for this is the whole duty of man.*"

Love and Judgment

It also showed that Adam and Eve did not love God nor abide in God's love. Yeshua said in John 14:15, "*If you love me, you will keep my commandments,*" and in John 15:10, "*If you keep my commandments, you will abide in my love, just as I have kept my Father's commandments and abide in his love.*"

Contrary to popular belief of professing Christians that God's love tolerates whatever they justify doing. God's love for humans is expressed in His commandments, which forbid as well as require certain works. Hebrews 12:6 says, "*For the Lord disciplines the one he loves, and chastises every son whom he receives.*"

So, if Eve rebuked the serpent, does that mean Eve did not love her neighbor? If Adam rebuked Eve and did not eat the forbidden fruit, does that mean Adam did not love his wife? Answer: Clearly not, if Adam and Eve do not want the death consequence for others just like they do not want for themselves. The serpent, however, wanted Adam and Eve to die by enticing them against God's commandment.

Did God not know what the serpent was doing? Was God unable to prevent Adam and Eve from disobeying Him? Answer: Absolutely not. God knew and allowed both acts of sinning to happen. God said in Jeremiah 17:10, "*I the Lord search the heart and test the mind, to give every man according to his ways, according to the fruit of his deeds.*"

When God asked Adam and Eve about their disobedient acts, Adam cited the presence and action of his wife, and Eve cited the deception from the serpent. These were indeed the catalysts for why they disobeyed God. However, these excuses also showed how Adam and Eve valued and trusted others, not God. And that external influence and being deceived do not excuse one from God's judgment.

So, did God force Adam and Eve to sin? Did Adam and Eve not have personal responsibility for their actions? Answer: Clearly not. God said in Genesis 4:7, "*If you do well, will you not be accepted? And if you do not do well, sin is crouching at the door. Its desire is contrary to you, but you must rule over it.*"

Subsequently, God carried out His judgments on Adam and Eve and drove them out of the Garden of Eden, which was the original kingdom of God made for them. They would have to suffer each in their own way and were indeed going to die by returning to dust.

It seemed they deserved to die immediately, but somehow, God let them live out a life before death. And this was done implicitly at the cost of an animal life, the first sacrifice and death since creation. So that its skin was used to cover Adam and Eve's nakedness during their lifetime.

Saved the Same Way

Adam and Eve had broken the covenant of obedience with God, and subsequently, God implemented the "covenant of salvation" just as He had planned beforehand. This was the unfolding of God's grace and mercy via His salvation plan for certain offspring of the woman. Right after the fall of Adam and Eve, the good news of the gospel had been revealed via God's spoken words directly to them and the serpent.

God carried out His judgment on the serpent and said in Genesis 3:15, "*I will put enmity between you and the woman and between your offspring and her offspring; he shall bruise your head, and you shall bruise his heel.*" There will be a male offspring of the woman who will be victorious over the serpent. Despite being in enmity and attacked by the serpent, He fights and deals damage to the serpent's critical organ.

Who the Victor is, and the details of the story unfolded over the course of history. He is Yeshua, the Messiah. **Yeshua is the eternal Word of God** that became flesh, as all Christians shall know. Any human, before and after His ministry on earth, if then is saved the same way by His works through faith in Him.

Believing in Yeshua means believing in what God said, not anyone else's to the contrary. All the words that came from the mouth of the

Father and of the Son, they are one. And people always live out what they truly believe, not what they claim to believe. How people live their lives is evidence of what they truly believe in. Just like Adam and Eve, what is evident of men not keeping the Father's commandments?

Abraham was saved by God because he truly believed and subsequently did exactly all God had told him regardless of the corresponding costs to him. The Law in Abraham's heart is what God had commanded him. God tested Abraham and commanded him to sacrifice his son Isaac. Abraham did not test God's words but was willing to do so. True children of Abraham are those who believe in and obey God's words.

Along with the Israelites who left Egypt during the ministry of Moses were a mixed multitude of people. These people were not descendants of Abraham, yet they believed and did what God said. They were accepted by God as His people under the same Law. Certain children of these people also entered God's promised land of Canaan after 40 years in the wilderness.

Rahab, a gentile prostitute, was saved and grafted into Israel long before Yeshua's ministry on earth. She truly believed what she heard the God of Israel had said and subsequently risked her life to be on God's side. If Rahab was willing to risk her life, what would stop her from obeying God's Law later in her life?

One could point out that Abraham and Rahab told lies in their stories. That's true, and they were not sinless, just like any other human. However, note that they lied to men whom they did not believe in while doing God's will. Undoubtedly, they must have repented of their sins in order to be saved later.

So, were Adam and Eve saved later? Answer: there is no partiality with God. If, after the fall, they had learned their lesson, always did all of God's words no matter the suffering, never believed and listened to anything to the contrary again until the day they died, then yes. They believed in Yeshua before His incarnation, which is what God said, which is the Word of God later became flesh and died for their sins.

The Father's Will

The popular Christian belief, that the will of the Father is to only intellectually believe in Yeshua, is another deception from the serpent. James 2:20-26 says, "*Do you want to be shown, you foolish person, that faith apart from works is useless? Was not Abraham our father justified by works when he offered up his son Isaac on the altar?... You see that a person is justified by works and not by faith alone....*"

A believer's works, which are tangible evidence for belief or disbelief in God, will be used for judgment before His great white throne. Revelation 20:12 says, "*...And the dead were judged by what was written in the books, according to what they had done.*" The Word of God in Luke 6:46 says, "*Why do you call me 'Lord, Lord,' and not do what I tell you?*"

During His ministry on earth, Yeshua taught to hear, learn and keep the word of the Father, which was Himself before His incarnation. Yeshua said in John 6:45, "*It is written in the Prophets, 'And they will all be taught by God.' Everyone who has heard and learned from the Father comes to me-,*" and in Luke 11:28, "*Blessed rather are those who hear the word of God and keep it!*"

Regarding the Law, Yeshua repeatedly stressed in Matthew 5:18, "*For truly, I say to you, until heaven and earth pass away, not an iota, not a dot, will pass from the Law until all is accomplished,*" and in Luke 16:17, "*But it is easier for heaven and earth to pass away than for one dot of the Law to become void.*"

Yeshua also taught us to do and teach the Law. Yeshua said in Matthew 5:19, "*Therefore whoever relaxes one of the least of these commandments and teaches others to do the same will be called least in the kingdom of heaven, but whoever does them and teaches them will be called great in the kingdom of heaven.*"

Yet, as of present-day in America's Christianity, when a believer keeps the Father's commandments, he is accused of working for salvation. And if he rejects the tradition of pagan practices, he is accused of falling from grace. What is wrong with God's previously spoken words? What is wrong with Yeshua, before or after His incarnation? Are Yeshua of Israel and Jesus of America not the same person?

If a believer is not doing God's commandments while claiming to have the security of salvation, then what works is the believer doing? And by doing works other than God's commandments, just because the works are called "for God," is God obligated to give him eternal life? This is actually the original definition of salvation by works (on one's own terms) in its historical context during Yeshua's ministry on earth.

To do God's commandments, a believer has to give up his own works and will, and give up what he had been doing in the past. Doing God's commandments is doing God's will. Sin is transgression of God's commandments, and turning from that to keep God's commandments is repentance. Keeping God's commandments and repentance are the same. And yet, many professing Christians do not see it. Why?

What's Wrong

Look at what is being taught in mainstream Christian schools and churches in America; Dispensational theology teaches that God treats Israel and the Christian church differently. Covenant theology teaches that God's new covenant of grace replaces His previous covenant of works. The former infers God's partiality; the latter infers God's changing His mind. And both infer no need to keep the Father's words.

Furthermore, they teach interpretations of scriptures to support these theologies, such as Jesus breaking the Sabbath and also declaring all foods clean; The Law has passed away, and gentile converts only have 4 specific requirements, according to the Jerusalem Council. Are they allowed to murder, steal, and lie? And if, in fact, these 4 requirements, isn't it still a law? Isn't it still salvation by works?

If a person rather trusts not in what the religious establishments teach but actually thinks for himself: God's partiality means 2 people who live the same way do the same works, but 1 will go to "Heaven" and 1 will go to "Hell." God's changing His mind means one day in the future, as it turns out, only the highest bidders for salvation or those who raised the most money in the name of Jesus will enter "Heaven."

When Yeshua rebuked the religious professionals of His day, **He rebuked them for not keeping the Law**. He said in John 7:19, "*Has not Moses given you the law? Yet none of you keeps the law. Why do you seek to kill me?*" Stephen also rebuked them for not keeping the Law in Acts 7:53, "*You who received the law as delivered by angels and did not keep it.*" Did these scribes and Pharisees work for their salvation at all?

Answer: Yes, they did work for salvation, but on their own terms. Because they did not believe in the Father's words, which were Yeshua before and after His incarnation, as delivered to them by Moses. The Word of God in John 5:46-47 says, "*For if you believed Moses, you would believe me; for he wrote of me. But if you do not believe his writings, how will you believe my words?*"

Rather, they believed in salvation through the made-up religious works and laws from their like-minded fathers. They were keeping the made-up tradition, not the Father's Law. The Word of God in Mark 7:9 says, "*You have a fine way of rejecting the commandment of God in order to establish your tradition!*"

They did so to unjustly benefit themselves, as they believed they were entitled to, while oppressing the marginalized. The Word of God in Matthew 23:4 says, "*They tie up heavy burdens, hard to bear, and lay them on people's shoulders, but they themselves are not willing to move them with their finger.*"

They made overly strict the appearance aspect of the Law while disobeying its spirit. The Word of God in Luke 11:42 says, "*But woe to you, Pharisees! For you tithe mint and rue and every herb, and neglect justice and the love of God. These you ought to have done without neglecting the others.*" Justice, love for God, and love for neighbor are God's laws that were missing in the practices of the religious professionals of Yeshua's day.

Yeshua's Teachings

The Father's words in Deuteronomy 6:5-6 says, "*You shall love the LORD your God with all your heart and with all your soul and with all your might. And these words that I command you today shall be on your heart,*" and in Deuteronomy 6:17 says, "*You shall diligently keep the commandments of the LORD your God, and his testimonies and his statutes, which he has commanded you.*"

The Father's words in Leviticus 19:18 says, "*You shall not take vengeance or bear a grudge against the sons of your own people, but you shall love your neighbor as yourself: I am the LORD,*" and in Leviticus 19:34 says, "*You shall treat the stranger who sojourns with you as the native among you, and you shall love him as yourself, for you were strangers in the land of Egypt: I am the LORD your God.*"

The scribes and Pharisees claimed to know and keep the Father's words. In reality, however, they mostly believed and kept what they heard from others, not the intent of the Father's words. So when Yeshua rebuked them, He repeatedly started with the phrase, "*You have heard that it was said,*" then He said, "*But I say to you.*" When Yeshua cited the Father's words, He repeatedly used the phrase "*It is written.*"

Yeshua did not teach or do anything contrary to the Father's words because the Father's words were Yeshua before His incarnation. Believers shall keep all of the Father's commandments, not just love their neighbor as themselves. **The commandments to love God and neighbor do not replace but are the spirit of the whole Law**. The Word of God in Matthew 22:40 says, "*On these two commandments depend all the Law and the Prophets.*"

If Yeshua Himself broke the Law and rebuked the scribes and Pharisees for not keeping the Law, wasn't He a hypocrite? If He declared all foods clean, didn't He abolish the Law contrary to what He claimed? By what Law is Yeshua sinless? If not, how can He be a lamb without blemish to make atonement for sins?

Biblical Deceptions

Now look at the same scripture in Mark 7:19 and compare between a modern ESV Bible, which I first learned from and used as a reference here, and an older KJV Bible. The ESV has "*(Thus he declared all foods clean)*" while the KJV has "*into the draught, purging all meats.*" Do they mean the same thing?

Examine the context of this scripture. Were Yeshua and the disciples eating unclean food, or eating bread which is clean food but with unwashed hands? What Yeshua was saying is that the digestive system purges all physical impurity in the eaten food, but the decision from the heart of a man defiles him.

Here is an illustrative example: If a believer refuses to ever eat any unclean food, but he is bound by the devil, and unclean food is forced down his throat into his stomach. So his stomach did digest the unclean food, and he violated the letter of the food law. The unclean food still cannot defile him in this case.

But if a believer was given the commandment from God not to eat the forbidden food but chose to believe in any explanation to the contrary of God's commandment and ate the food, then his decision to become unfaithful and disbelieve in God's previously spoken words, which was Yeshua, defiled him.

The text "*(Thus he declared all foods clean)*" is an added interpretation originated from the devil to deceive, exactly like it was in the Garden of Eden. And there are multiple other questionable or missing verses in the Bible, just by comparing ESV and KJV: 1 John 5:7-8, Acts 8:37, 9:5-6, 15:34, and 24:6-8. The genealogy recorded in Matthew and Luke differs and actually is the genealogy of Joseph, not of Yeshua.

Peter's vision, as described in Acts 10:9-16, is also misleadingly used as evidence for God's abolishment of the food law. Again, if a person rather trusts not in what the religious establishments teach but actually reads for himself: Peter's own interpretation of the vision is about person, not food, as recorded in Acts 10:28, "*...but God has shown me that I should not call any person common or unclean.*"

My point is this: God allows trials, temptations, errors, and deceptions to test the hearts and minds of all believers, just as what occurred to Adam and Eve, Job, Abraham, Solomon, Yeshua, and others. Do you truly believe in God's previously spoken words and keep them? Or Jesus and some scriptures have voided His words?

Deceptions through altering original scriptures and interpretations do not even compare to what more is coming in the last days. The Word of

God in Matthew 24:24 says, "*For false christs and false prophets will arise and perform great signs and wonders, so as to lead astray, if possible, even the elect.*" How do you know these christs and prophets are frauds? Answer: They contradict God's previously spoken words.

Paul is Not God

One could still object to the above. How about what Paul said in Romans 14:20, "*...Everything is indeed clean...*" and in 1 Corinthians 6:12, "*...All things are lawful for me...?*" Answer: This is what Paul also said in Romans 3:31, "*Do we then overthrow the law by this faith? By no means! On the contrary, we uphold the law.*" Apparently, Paul contradicts himself and multiple times so, as recorded in the scriptures.

What Paul said is what Paul said, is Paul the eternal Word of God like Yeshua? Does Paul have the authority to overwrite God's previously spoken words? Was Paul without errors and sins? If indeed Paul said anything contrary to God's words, then the devil was speaking through him. The idea that the Bible is the Word of God is a deception to elevate any scripture equal to words that came from God's mouth.

To be clear, I agree with all of Paul's messages in the context that what he said must submit to what God's previously said, both the Father's and Yeshua's words, they are one. God's main mission for Paul wasn't to baptize but to preach the gospel to the non-Jews and then support these early communities of converts. So that from the mass of these, some may later fully repent in accordance with God's words and be saved.

These believers are "infants" in the faith who were not ready for real spiritual discipline and needed much grace and learning. Paul said in 1 Corinthians 3:1-2, "*But I, brothers, could not address you as spiritual people, but as people of the flesh, as infants in Christ. I fed you with milk, not solid food, for you were not ready for it. And even now, you are not yet ready.*"

Understand that before his conversion, not very long time previously, Paul (Saul) was a prominent Pharisee who practiced the Pharisees' law and traditions, not God's Law. Paul said in Galatians 1:14, "*And I was advancing in Judaism beyond many of my own age among my people, so extremely zealous was I for the traditions of my fathers.*"

Paul witnessed the rebuttal from Stephen and approved of his execution. Acts 7:58 tells, "*Then they cast him out of the city and stoned him. And the witnesses laid down their garments at the feet of a young man named Saul.*" Acts 8:1-3 tells, "*And Saul approved of his execution...But Saul was ravaging the church....*"

After being supernaturally rebuked by Yeshua, which is the Word of God, Paul's eyes were opened to the truth. The Word who faithfully lived out all of God's words His whole life, even unto death, was resurrected and anointed Lord of all. Paul and everyone else had lived in transgressions and eventually shall die without redemption. But by the atonement of Yeshua, people can work out their own salvation.

The Only Way

When the Word of God said in John 14:6, "*I am the way, and the truth, and the life. No one comes to the Father except through me.*" He means living out all of God's words like He does is the way, the truth, and the life. No one comes to the Father except through living out all of God's words like He does. How the Word of God lived His life is the perfect example for a believer to live out all of God's words.

Animals sacrificed for sins only spare sinners from immediate execution according to the Law but not eventual death; because essentially God had said sinners must die. So, for a sinner to still have a way to eternal life, the very eternal Word of God must be sacrificed. However, the Word of God did not die and was no more, but lives again forevermore. And sinners have a second chance to comply with God's words.

In the same way as in the past, when Moses came back from Mount Sinai for the first time, he broke the stone tablets because the Israelites were living contrary to God's words written on them. When Moses came back from Mount Sinai the second time, he brought the new stone tablets with the exact same God's words written on them. And from that point on, God's words were enforced on the Israelites.

There are no new terms in the "new covenant," but the same covenant is renewed because of God's grace with a grace period to enforce when the Word of God returns. The covenant terms have always been wholeheartedly living out all of God's previously spoken words. Only when extraordinary external forces are against a believer's will, like persecution, that he may externally fail to fulfill God's words.

Upholding the Law

The thief on the cross next to Yeshua was justified through faith is a good example to illustrate why the external performance of the Law is not the means for salvation. Understand that the thief confessed he deserved crucifixion, was just waiting to die soon, and could not possibly do anything even if he wanted to. If the thief had been released to live, undoubtedly, he would seek God's words to live out even unto death.

God's will for humans since Adam has always been to believe in God and, therefore, do what God said. Believing in a code of conduct like the Law is not the same as believing in God, even if the Law was encoded from what God said. Believing in the Law for salvation means salvation is achieved by successfully performing the Law regardless of anything else. It's like the Law becomes a god giving salvation to whoever performs to it.

True believers have the spirit of the Law written on their hearts, not the letter of the Law written on stone tablets and scrolls. It's the spirit that motivates believers, not external conformance. A marriage of many decades without anyone cheating performs to the letter of the Law. However, if the couple lost the initial love and hated each other, then they violated the spirit of marriage as intended by God.

No human can be justified by the Law because all have already failed to comply with the Law. One does not have to continuously violate the Law to be guilty. One time violation in the past is guilty and shall be executed accordingly. However, one is justified through faith in what God said, which changed the heart from transgressing to upholding the Law. This internal upholding of the Law manifests externally into actions.

Yeshua came to be baptized by John the Baptist is a good example to illustrate how internal upholding always manifests externally. Baptism by itself is only symbolic; however, if a person disregards this ordinance, then it shows the person's unrighteousness toward God. Yeshua explained this to John the Baptist in Matthew 3:15, "*Let it be so now, for thus it is fitting for us to fulfill all righteousness.*"

Even though baptism is not in the Law, it was implicit in the scriptures that: Noah and his family were saved through water; the Israelites were baptized into Moses in the cloud and in the sea; Jonah passed from death to life via three days in the depth of the sea; Elijah and Elisha passed through the waters of the Jordan. Yeshua upheld and performed all righteousness, including those not explicitly written in the Law.

For these reasons, in his letters to the non-Jew converts, Paul fought hard against imposing any external performance of the Law as a requirement for salvation, yet he insisted on upholding the Law at the same time. Paul said in Galatians 6:13, "*For even those who are circumcised do not themselves keep the law, but they desire to have you circumcised that they may boast in your flesh,*" and in Romans 2:13,

"For it is not the hearers of the law who are righteous before God, but the doers of the law who will be justified."

Proper Context

To properly understand Paul's messages, one needs to understand the context of his letters. The non-Jew converts originally had little to no concept of the Law and practiced various forms of idolatry and false religion that they needed to repent from. These converts themselves were the minority among their existing people and culture. After the initial conversion, they started to learn more about the Law.

The minority non-Jew converts were questioned by their majority existing people and culture for their "strange" visible practice of the Law. Contrary to popular Christian teachings today, Paul, in fact, defended their practice of the Law when he said in Colossians 2:16, "*Therefore let no one pass judgment on you in questions of food and drink, or with regard to a festival or a new moon or a Sabbath.*"

Then Paul proceeded to defend them from the discrimination and false religious practice of their majority existing people and culture. Paul said in Colossians 2:18, "*Let no one disqualify you, insisting on asceticism and worship of angels, going on in detail about visions...*" Later, Paul also stressed the proper use of the Law in 1 Timothy 1:8, "*Now we know that the law is good, if one uses it lawfully.*"

Both the Jew and non-Jew converts were living contrary to God's words encoded in the Law, just like non-believers. And the atonement for sins of the Word of God effectively spares the whole world from God's immediate judgment. So Paul made sure the non-Jew converts received this grace also. This does not mean they were not living in sin, nor there will not be God's final judgment.

For the same reasons, the Jerusalem Council concluded not to impose the Law on the non-Jew converts but advised them of their popular sins: things polluted by idols, sexual immorality, what has been strangled, and blood. A believer would need to study all of God's words to know all that are sins. By the end of Paul's ministry, most of the non-Jew converts did not endure and already fell away.

One Teacher, Few Chosen

Salvation only comes from the Word of God, not the words of Paul or any other apostles. One can be converted without knowing the works of Paul and the apostles. By his own account, Paul said in Romans 16:7, "*Greet Andronicus and Junia..., and they were in Christ before me,*" and in 2 Corinthians 12:2, "*I know a man in Christ who fourteen years ago was caught up to the third heaven..., God knows.*"

And initial conversion does not equal salvation, not at all. One's conversion only indicates the person was called and responded positively to a certain extent. The Word of God explained through the parable of the sower that those who hear the words and receive them with joy but do not endure tribulation nor prove fruitful are not chosen people of God. He said in Matthew 22:14, "*For many are called, but few are chosen.*"

In the parable of the wedding feast, there are many invited to the Kingdom of heaven, but those who came without wedding garments were cast out. In the parable of the ten virgins, all of them were seeking the bridegroom, but those who took no oil with them were denied. Those believers are not chosen because they failed to properly prepare themselves according to what God expected of them.

The main role of the apostles is to direct believers to the Word of God without modifying, qualifying, or overwriting. The Word of God in Matthew 23:8-10 says, "*But you are not to be called rabbi, for you have one teacher, and you are all brothers...Neither be called instructors, for you have one instructor, the Christ.*" A believer shall discern if a teaching is fully compliant with what God previously said.

Sabbath Rest

The Sabbath is a holy day since God's creation of the world, regardless of whether a person observes it or not. Genesis 2:3 tells, "*So God blessed the seventh day and made it holy...*" During the early human days of Cain and Abel, no scriptures indicated any God's law they needed to obey, yet Cain and Abel made offerings to God. Both were externally religious, but Cain committed murder and was punished by God.

God instituted the Sabbath, the Passover, and other feasts because they matter. Each nation on earth has its unique history and national holidays, and God's kingdom also has its unique history and holy days. A citizen of a country observes the nation's unique special days, not that of another nation. Seek first the kingdom of God means to seek first the kingdom's King, law, values, and ways of life.

When the Word of God said in Matthew 11:28-30, "*Come to me, all who labor and are heavy laden, and I will give you rest...*" He was calling all people who are busy with their own way of life they shall obey and learn from Him. Their souls can rest from their worries of life, and the burden of obeying Him is light. So believers shall rest on the Sabbath according to the Word of God, not in their own way.

The popular Christian interpretation, that because Yeshua is the Sabbath rest then the weekly Sabbath rest has been made void, is another deception and a logical fallacy. This interpretation says: $(Y = \text{true}, Y = S) \rightarrow S = \text{false}$, which is wrong, and the correct deduction shall be $S = \text{true}$. Believers shall rest on the weekly Sabbath to honor Yeshua. All the Sabbaths in the Law and the millennial Sabbath in the future shall be honored.

No Excuses

If a believer starts to recognize he is living contrary to any of God's words, is there any excuse for him to stay that way, or shall he deny himself and change his way? The Word of God is clear that no worldly reasons, only losing his own life for God's words, shall be an excuse. He said in Matthew 10:37-39, "*Whoever loves father or mother more than me is not worthy of me..., and whoever loses his life for my sake will find it.*"

The Word of God in Matthew 7:21 says, "*Not everyone who says to me, 'Lord, Lord,' will enter the kingdom of heaven, but the one who does the will of my Father who is in heaven.*" And Paul also said in Hebrews 10:26, "*For if we go on sinning deliberately after receiving the knowledge of the truth, there no longer remains a sacrifice for sins.*"

One could question, by upholding the Law, shall believers perform sacrifices and offerings? Answer: Yes, of course. However, understand that Yeshua's sacrifice for sins is still in effect since the day He died on the cross and only ends when He returns. The body of chosen believers is the current temple of God, where believers shall sacrifice to offer services to God, to do all of God's words.

A believer shall uphold the Law to the fullest of his current resource and capability and work toward being increasingly dependent on God. When Yeshua returns and reigns as the King of kings on earth at the literal temple of God in Jerusalem, chosen believers will be allotted specific land for inheritance so that they can grow and make full sacrifices and offerings according to the Law.

Finally, because Satan is the current god of this world, he is in control of all the resources and powers to deceive, tempt, or coerce people to live contrary to God's words. Besides personal sins that a believer can repent, most people are also living dependent on the devil's sinful systems. So, to live a truly holy life dependent on God only, the believer will inevitably clash with the establishments and be persecuted.

Acronyms and Abbreviations

401(k) ....Retirement plan that allows employees to contribute a portion of their wages to individual account

ABET ....Accreditation Board for Engineering and Technology

ANAC ....Anacor Pharmaceuticals, Inc

ARC ....Association Retreat Center

ASF ....alt. seduction. fast

AutoCAD ....Computer-aided design and drafting software application

B-52 ....Boeing B-52 Stratofortress, an American long-range, subsonic, jet-powered strategic bomber

BBC ....Bethlehem Baptist Church

BP ....British Petroleum

CD ....Compact Disc

CEO ....Chief Executive Officer

CFA ....Chartered Financial Analyst

CFP ....Certified Financial Planner

CMT ....Chartered Market Technician

CN ....Canadian National

COVID-19 ....Coronavirus disease 2019

CT ....Computed Tomography

Dr. ....Doctor

EB-2 Visa ....Employment-based immigration, second preference

EFI ....Engineering and Fire Investigation

EIT ....Engineer In Training

ESV ....English Standard Version

F-1 Visa ....(Academic Student) allows you to enter the United States as a full-time student at an accredited academic institution

FE ....Fundamental of Engineering

FIFA ....Fédération Internationale de Football Association

FINRA ....Financial Industry Regulatory Authority

Form I-20 ....Certificate of Eligibility for Nonimmigrant Student Status

GPA ....Grade Point Average

GPS ....Global Positioning System

GRE ....Graduate Record Exam

H-1B Visa ....Nonimmigrant classification applies to workers in a specialty occupation

HCC ....Hope Community Church

HCMC ....Hennepin County Medical Center

ISBN ....International Standard Book Number

J-1 Visa ....(Exchange Visitors) is for educational and cultural exchange programs

JD ....Juris Doctor

KJV ....King James Version

LDS ....Latter-day Saints

Mathcad ....Computer software for the verification, documentation, and use of mathematical calculations

MBA ....Master of Business Administration

MCEER ....Multidisciplinary Center for Earthquake Engineering Research

Mr. ....Mister

MRI ....Magnetic Resonance Imaging

MTA ....Market Technicians Association

NCEES ....National Council of Examiners for Engineering and Surveying

NDE ....Near-Death Experience

NHTC ....Natural Health Trends Corp

NIV ....New International Version

NLNK ....NewLink Genetics Corporation

OPT ....Optional Practical Training

P.E. ....Professional Engineer

PC ....Personal Computer

PE ....Principles and Practice of Engineering

Ph.D. ....Doctor of Philosophy

PMD ....Practice Management Development

RBC ....Royal Bank of Canada

Risa-3D ....Rapid Interactive Structural Analysis 3 Dimensional

SPEAK ....Speaking Proficiency English Assessment Kit

SSN ....Social Security Number

SUNY ....State University of New York

TIN ....Taxpayer Identification Number

TOEFL ....Test of English as a Foreign Language

TV ....Television

U of M ....University of Minnesota

U.S. ....United States

UBS ....Union Bank of Switzerland

UK ....United Kingdom

UNLV ....University of Nevada, Las Vegas

USD ....United States Dollar

VEF ....Vietnam Education Foundation

VGSA ....Vietnamese Graduate Student Association

Made in the USA
Monee, IL
14 June 2024

fa546d4a-637b-4ab8-9972-c6bfa5c6fa5aR01